Handbook of the New Thought

How the Power of Thought
Can Change Your Life and
Heal the Body, Mind and Spirit

Handbook of the New Thought

How the Power of Thought Can Change Your Life and Heal the Body, Mind and Spirit

by

Horatio W. Dresser

Edited and Updated for the 21st century
by
William F. Shannon

Hudson Mohawk Press
Latham, NY

Hudson Mohawk Press
595 New Loudon Road #138
Latham, New York 12110

www.hudsonmohawkpress.com
www.facebook.com/hudsonmohawkpress

Editing, updating and introduction
copyright © 2013 by Hudson Mohawk Press

All rights reserved.

This edited and updated edition first published in the United States in 2013 by Hudson Mohawk Press. *Handbook of the New Thought* was previously published in different form in 1917 by The Knickerbocker Press of G.P. Putnam's Sons, New York.

The text of this updated edition has been edited into gender neutral language, except when to do so would render the text awkward for the reader.

ISBN 978-0-98430407-3 (paperback)
eISBN 978-0-9843040-8-0

Library of Congress Control Number: 2013935250

Book design by William F. Shannon

CONTENTS

Introduction to the 2013 Edition   i

Foreword to the 1917 Edition   v

Chapter One
Exposition   1

Chapter Two
Historical Sketch   17

Chapter Three
The Silent Method   33

Chapter Four
Estimate   59

Chapter Five
The Mental Theory of Disease   79

Chapter Six
Reconstruction   103

Chapter Seven
Practical Suggestions   125

INTRODUCTION TO THE 2013 EDITION

by
William F. Shannon

Handbook of the New Thought by Horatio W. Dresser is a valuable resource for anyone with a desire to put into practice metaphysical ideas such as the law of attraction, affirmations, meditation, mental healing of the body, and mind treatment. It is for anyone who wants to change their life in any way. In clear language this book explains how the power of thought can be used to heal the body, mind and spirit, and thus eliminate fear, anxiety, worry, nervousness, pessimism and unbelief. Everyone can benefit from reading it. Dresser explains clearly what New Thought is and how it arose in the 1800s. As he says, New Thought is "a philosophy of the inner life which can be applied to all problems and needs" and this book "is intended as a guide to daily life." It is a great resource for those just starting to learn about New Thought, and for those who want to learn more.

Dresser's explanations of New Thought ideas and concepts are especially interesting for two reasons. First, Dresser was a major figure in the movement as discussed below. Second, even though he was a major figure he did not shy away from criticizing things about New Thought that he thought were unhelpful or just plain wrong. This evenhandedness gives his story of the history and uses of New Thought more weight. He does not tell the story with rose-colored glasses. He has looked at both sides and yet he still comes out clearly on the side that says the power of the mind is the most important asset each of us has. It doesn't matter if you are rich or poor, male or female, or where you live or anything else, each person has this great asset -- the power to change their thinking and thus change their life. Yes, we all find ourselves in particular circumstances that may appear to be holding us back for whatever reason, but we still have the awesome power to decide how to respond to those circumstances with our thoughts and actions. We can always affect the outcome. We always have choices. Often we forget just how much power that fact truly gives us. Dresser reminds us eloquently in this book, over and over again, just how important it is to remember this truth.

Handbook of the New Thought has been unavailable in either print or digital form for many years, making it much less known than Dresser's *History of the New Thought Movement* that was first published two years after the *Handbook* in 1919. Indeed, few public libraries have a circulating copy of the original edition of *Handbook of the New Thought* in their collection. The fact that the book has been hidden for so long is a great pity because the volume retains its relevance today. Aside from some dated passages and specific references to Dresser's particular time and place, in many ways the book could have been written yesterday. Dresser's style is

Introduction

crisp and clear and the reader will recognize in the text many of the same New Thought ideas and concepts still widely discussed today, like the law of attraction, affirmations, meditation, and mind treatment.

Chapter Seven ("Practical Suggestions") is especially useful for the reader today, even as it was almost 100 years ago when Dresser first wrote it. Anyone who wants to put New Thought ideas and concepts to practical use will benefit by reading *Handbook of the New Thought*. Dresser's discussion of how many of the ideas of early 20th century psychologists such as Sigmund Freud and William James are compatible with New Thought teachings also retains it relevance today, as people try to reconcile an increasingly deterministic view of psychology with the more intuitive spiritual inclinations of humanity that sometimes defy "scientific" explanation, and will not go away no matter how much some "professionals" try to ignore them. New Thought provides a way to reconcile these seemingly irreconcilable attitudes.

This edition of *Handbook of the New Thought* is edited into gender neutral language to make it even more accessible to a 21st century audience. Please enjoy this updated edition of an important and powerful New Thought classic.

* * * * *

Horatio W. Dresser (1866–1954) was a major leader in the New Thought movement. It is safe to say that Dresser grew up steeped in New Thought. His parents, Julius and Annetta Seabury Dresser, studied in New England with Phineas Parkhurst Quimby

(1802-1866), the man to whom the origin of the New Thought movement is generally traced. Dresser was admitted to Harvard in 1891, but dropped out in 1893 when his father died; he returned to Harvard in 1903 and completed his Ph.D. in 1907. In 1919, Dresser became a minister in the General Convention of the Church of the New Jerusalem, a denomination based on the teaching of Emanuel Swedenborg (1688-1772), and briefly served as a pastor of a Swedenborgian church in Portland, Maine. Dresser discusses in several parts of *Handbook of the New Thought* how the New Thought movement is indebted to the spiritual ideas of Swedenborg. In 1921, Dresser compiled Quimby's manuscripts and made them available to readers in full for the first time. Dresser's compilation was important in showing that even Mary Baker Eddy's Christian Science movement can be traced back to Quimby, notwithstanding Christian Science's protestations to the contrary. Dresser died on March 30, 1954 in Boston, Massachusetts.

* * * * *

WILLIAM F. SHANNON is the Publisher and Editor of Hudson Mohawk Press. He holds a Master of Arts in Integrated Studies/Cultural Studies from Athabasca University in Canada.

PREFACE TO THE 1917 EDITION

The New Thought stands for the affirmative attitude. It affirms success even amidst failure. It endeavors to compass the whole of life, and to show that there are inner resources for every possible need or occasion. It stands for the power of mind in contrast with the alleged supremacy of environment. It stands for the opportunities of the present in contrast with heredity. It makes for the elimination of fear, anxiety, worry, nervousness, excitement, depression, pessimism, unbelief. It is a vigorous gospel of health and healing. It is constructive, positive, optimistic; believes in the supremacy of the good, the triumph of ideals, the development of productive individuality. Its clue to the spiritual life is found through meditation, realization, service through emphasis on inner peace and poise; and it fosters belief in the immediate, immanent presence of God as our Spirit Source.

Thus challenging the attention as a philosophy of the inner life which can be applied to all problems and needs, the New Thought has not yet borne the test of definition, comparison, and systematization.* It has not been tested by the scientific method. No attempt has been made to assign its methods to an appropriate place in relation to the methods of other types of practical thought. Thus far its theory of disease has passed without careful examination.

This book at least makes a beginning in this direction. Its conclusions have borne the test of many years of investigation. The aim is to be analytical, and in a measure critical, but not too critical The results aimed at are practical, hence the book ends with suggestions for immediate use, and it is intended as a guide to daily life.

The author has undertaken this estimate because, while deeply interested in the subjects under consideration, he stands in a measure apart from any branch of the mental healing movement. Mental healing as a movement is apt to run into fads and other side-issues. It tends to become a method of "demonstrating over" all events and conditions, as if the entire cosmos were plastic to thought. In extreme form, it tends to foster the idea that a person's consciousness may rightfully become "all ego." Thus its devotees are often blind to the lessons which facts teach. But it need not be carried to the extreme, may profit by the lessons of life, and find a wiser method of attaining spiritual supremacy. There should be a way to draw upon the resources of the inner life and adopt the affirmative attitude without indulging in any

---

* Dresser is writing in 1917 before there was a comprehensive view of the nature, history and aims of the New Thought movement.

illusions concerning suggestion, the subconscious, the "subjective mind," or any other special idea or interpretation. Thus the New Thought should pass out of its reactionary stage, and find its place amidst other tendencies of thought seeking a rational place in our time.

There are various signs that this change is in process, hence that the time has come for rational estimates. Formerly it was difficult to bring together the representatives of the movement into any kind of productive organization. Now[†] there is a successful international alliance in affiliation with the various centers, local societies, and clubs; and holding representative conventions. It is therefore more readily possible for the onlooker to state the common tendencies with fairness, also to point out some of the fallacies and results to be avoided. In this larger sense of the word the New Thought is only one of various tendencies which seek to emancipate the individual, and point the way to the regeneration of society. In this sense, too, it may be said to have a contribution to make to the new age ushered in by the great world war.[‡] Thus in brief it stands for "God in us," in contrast with the former idea of "God with us," or "God outside of the world." It stands for inner resources and claims that these are supreme. This book is accordingly offered as a guide to all who wish to test this claim.

[†] Dresser is speaking of the situation in 1917.

[‡] Dresser is referring to World War One, also known until 1939 as the Great War, the major war that took place between 1914 and 1918.

CHAPTER ONE

Exposition

In undertaking a study of the New Thought it is well to note that we are to be concerned with practical ideas and methods, not with a theory as the term is understood in the scientific world. Hence we should neither look for scientific definitions nor judge by traditional standards. The matters before us may be regarded by themselves, in the light of their use, whatever views we may chance to hold on theological grounds. If we prejudge we are likely to miss the practical meaning. But if we apply the tests of experience, following experience where it leads, we may discover a rich field of truth, new resources and new powers.

What we need to gain is a certain point of view. We need to disengage our thought for the time being from the ordinary round of activities, especially those implying the assumption that a person is merely a body with a soul, and take up the viewpoint of the inner life. Regarded in this way, a person is a soul or spirit, while the body is simply the vehicle of expression, the means of interchange with the outward world. The inner life as thus regarded is the realm of causes, of efficient beliefs and attitudes. To acquire this point of view is to begin to investigate the true meaning of life.

This study is in a sense unlike any other, for one does not depend on creed or authority. It is a study of life itself. We all possess this thing called "life" and all may observe and learn from it. For it is the stream of activity each moment pulsating within us, the "stream of thought" by which we learn that we the observers exist in the world, and by which we learn that the observer is different from the things observed. Our knowledge in this direction is measured only by our own efforts to investigate. Nothing can keep us from the truth if we really wish to learn. This whole wondrous world of the inner life is ours for the asking. The investigation begins the moment we think about life for ourselves as lovers of truth, ready to be guided by the wisdom of life.

Definition. The New Thought is a convenient term for a practical mode of taking life, wider in scope and content than the term itself implies, and is best understood in the light of the beliefs and methods which it represents. The term has gradually taken the place of "Mental Science," "The New Metaphysical Movement," "Metaphysical Healing, " and other names for mental healing other than Christian Science, the Emmanuel Movement, and Psychotherapy (the scientific term for mental healing). The teaching in question is not now limited to the theory and practice of healing, but involves a view of life as a whole. Its wider meanings have grown out of the method of silent healing, however, and it may be most intelligently defined if put in comparison with other terms expressing faith in the power of the spirit over the flesh in health and disease.

New Thought and Christian Science. These two terms have various points in common, and some of the followers of the New Thought owe their first interest in mental healing to Christian Science. Christian Science as a movement of thought, however, differs from the New Thought because of its mode of organization and its text-book, the work of a leader, Mary Baker Eddy, recognized as an authority. It differs also on account of its more radical views of matter, disease, and other points involved in the theory known as a "science" and distinguished from exact science by its "key to the Scriptures." One may assimilate its practical teachings and apply them for oneself, apart from the views peculiar to the "science." These teachings may be re-stated in the language of psychology, without reference to the interpretations of Scripture. Thus "mental" as opposed to "Christian" science is a practical method and theory of healing based on the authority of experience, rather than the authority of any leader or book. The term "Mental Science" was first employed in this way in 1882. It has since given place to other terms. But the idea that there is a "spiritual science" which may be stated without any reference to the doctrine known as "Christian Science" is still shared by many advocates of the New Thought.

New Thought and the Emmanuel Movement. The Emmanuel Movement is of recent origin,[§] and was organized to counteract Christian Science. Although in alliance with the Episcopal Church, its founders did not take their clues from the religious or Christian life in general. Nor did they fraternize with the New Thought. Their starting-point was that of scientific psychology of the sort which acknowledges the existence of the mind only so far as related to and conditioned by the brain. The practice starts with the diagnosis of disease by well-recognized physicians, and is limited to cases pronounced eligible in accordance with such diagnosis, that is, to cases of nervous and functional disease. The New Thought implies a different type of "mental science," presently to be considered. It is not dependent on scientific diagnosis, and does not recognize the customary distinctions between kinds of disease. The Emmanuel Movement can best be understood in connection with a study of psychotherapy and the more recent therapy employing psychoanalysis after the manner of Freud and his school. Advocates of such therapy would classify the New Thought as "unscientific."

New Thought and Hypnotism. The practice of hypnotism is usually confined to devotees of psychotherapy as employed in Europe and the United States.[**] It involves "hypnosis," a form of sleep in which the mind is open to "suggestion" or an idea intended to produce a given effect on mind and body after the hypnosis has ceased and an appointed time has elapsed. Such suggestions or ideas are affirmed by the practitioner with a view to influencing the

---

[§] Dresser is making this statement in 1917.

[**] This was Dresser's view of the situation in 1917.

Exposition

patient's mind. The patient's will plays little part in the process save in the act of yielding to the state called hypnosis. The after-effect occurs independently of the patient's co-operation. To all this the advocate of the New Thought objects on the ground that the patient should be educated, not insidiously influenced. Suggestion is employed by all schools of mental healing, but New Thought healers prefer to use it in the sense of an ideal offered to the intelligence of the patient, and without the use of hypnosis. The "silence" into which the recipient of mental treatment is invited to enter may seem similar to hypnosis, but it would have the equivalent influence only in case it were used by a therapist without principle. The spiritual method which we are presently to consider is very far removed from hypnotism. Suggestion as the common factor in all modes of mental treatment may be intelligently investigated entirely apart from the study of hypnotism.

Authorities. There is no book containing an adequate statement of all that the New Thought people believe. Hundreds of books and pamphlets have been issued since the movement spread throughout the world. These involve various interpretations and individual interests, and indicate the wide diversity of beliefs represented by the term. The best course for the student is to seek the principles which appeal to reason and bear the test of experience. Like the leaders of the New Thought, we may claim the right to think for ourselves, even if we depart from some of the teachings. Some of the leaders have retained their connection with the mainstream denominations, while others have organized Sunday meetings of their own. Still others have discovered leanings toward spiritism, theosophy, socialism, mysticism, pantheism, and the like. The movement is nothing if not broad and liberal. Under these conditions it could hardly be confined to any system, although related to liberalism in general.

The present exposition is based on the teachings of the writers of all branches of the movement. The aim is to state the cardinal principles so that they may be understood and applied in their own right. Thus one may avoid the tendency evinced in some quarters to ally the movement with Christian Science, hence to check inquiry. One may instead join those who, profiting by criticism, endeavor to make use of recent studies of the human mind. The direct clue is found through a study of the history of the movement. We might not reach the same results were we to begin to study the mind in relation to health as the investigation began more than sixty years ago. But we cannot interpret the ideas and methods sympathetically from within unless we learn how they came to be adopted. To take up the historical point of view is not necessarily to maintain that the earliest views were the most sound. But it is the earlier that explain the later views. This approach is particularly important in the case of a line of thought that has grown out of practical experience, not out of scientific theories or theories said to bear the authority of revelation.

The Old and the New. Although the New Thought is chiefly a working theory of mental healing, it has been extended to cover practical life as a whole, to include religion and philosophy, also a view of human society. We may therefore approach the subject at large before considering its special history. It is essentially "new" because it stands for a reaction, just

Exposition

as Protestantism was a reaction against the authority of the Roman Catholic Church.

The "old" thought against which the "new" reacts is any form of authority, whether medical or ecclesiastical, in so far as physicians and churches keep people in subjection to creeds. It is in particular a protest against materialism in all its forms. It objects to the notion that a person is a physical being, to be treated as if their soul played little or no part in their experience, in health and disease. It objects to the supposition that everyone is likely to go through a round of diseases, from childhood to old age, culminating in weakness and an untimely death. It objects, too, to most forms of medical practice, particularly the use of drugs, or any method of treatment based on a study of symptoms in contrast with inner causes.

In the sphere of the mainstream Christian churches, it objects to Calvinism and all other forms of orthodoxy implying emphasis on the sinfulness of humanity, on an atoning sacrifice, and a future punishment. It reacts against creeds and rituals in favor of a simpler interpretation of the Scriptures, simpler forms of worship, and belief in inner guidance. It substitutes silence or spiritual meditation for public prayer, and places emphasis on "realization" or actual experience and feeling instead of on "belief." Thus attention is called to the inner life of each individual, to present experience. All important changes or reforms are said to begin within, in the individual's thought and mental attitude. Thus its chief law is that of change or growth "from within outward." In the inner world of the self all resources are found, the basis of health, happiness, and success.

The reaction against authority was not a moderate one, but emphatic and complete. Most partisans of the new way of thinking ceased to employ physicians of any sort, and have since depended on mental healers or their own methods of self-help. Most of them also gave up organized religion altogether, although there has been a more recent tendency to return to the churches or to join one of the numerous societies holding Sunday services, such as the "Homes of Truth," the churches of the "Higher Life," "Divine Science," or the "Higher Thought."

The protest against medical authority was such that mental healers have ventured to treat diseases of all types with only the preparation that experience in this new field affords. It would be easier to condemn this venture than to appreciate the reasons for it. It implies a reaction against all external judgments or methods of diagnosis in favor of belief in intuition and inner receptivity, together with the clues made known by actual experience in mental healing. Regular instruction in the New Thought has long been given. But the first teachers learned by experience. Most of the leaders have continued to protest against the special sciences as "materialistic."

The New Thought claims to reveal life as a whole in a new light; that is, from the point of view of mental influences, states of consciousness and subconsciousness, social atmospheres, inner attitudes, expectations, and beliefs. To gain this new consciousness you should look within, dwelling upon the human spirit or soul from the point of view of the ideal. You should not only cease to think of yourself as a body with a soul, but dispense with your former world of thought, in so far as you regarded yourself as a creature of circumstance, subject to various diseases and evils of physical origin. Beginning to think of yourself as a spirit using the body as an instrument, you will presently realize that the real conditions in which you are placed are not imposed on you from without but bear intimate relation to your state of development. From this point on you will gain the new vision, phase by phase.

This world, for example, is not a hostile field, in which warring forces prey upon you without any relation to your interior states, but is a universe of law and order, a true unity or system. There is no evil as an independent reality contending with the good and in danger of overwhelming the human race. Nor is there any such entity as "disease" existing independently and attacking people, whatever their condition. Neither disease nor evil is attributable to our Creator. God made us to be good. God meant us to be healthy, and has provided all the conditions and forces essential to the maintenance of health. Our troubles are of our own making, through ignorance and a wrong attitude towards life. Therefore each person should look within, begin to realize the power of favorable beliefs, expectations, hope, good cheer; in contrast with fear, depression, doubt, and a negative attitude. The true philosophy of life is an abounding optimism, free in spirit, practical, affirmative; one that inspires an attitude favorable to the spiritual conditions of health, happiness, prosperity. The person who understands how they created their misery should be able to heal themselves by turning to the sources of life and power. Hence the first consideration is the changed point of view which gives this line of thought its character; the next is the practical method in which emphasis is placed on silence, affirmation, realization, the therapeutic practice of the presence of God.

The "old" thought emphasized the sovereignty of God, and looked upon humans as a miserably unfortunate creatures; the "new" dwells rather on the splendid powers and noble possibilities of each person. The old conception of humanity was that of relatively depraved beings, suffering for the sins of their first parents, and needing salvation from their own sins; the new emphasizes the native goodness of each person, and has little to say about sin. The former emphasis was upon the hard conditions of human existence, those that seemed to prove determinism; while the new emphasis is upon freedom. It was customary in terms of the outworn view to paint the miseries of this our natural existence, the horrors of hell, and the darker aspects of life in general; but the new picture is essentially cheerful, affirmative, ideal. The new has little or nothing to say about suffering, pain, or sorrow; little about sacrifice, the atonement, or salvation through the acceptance of the cross; and little about heredity, environment, or other supposed "limitations." The tendency is to break down all doctrinal barriers, adverse beliefs, and all exclusive distinctions; and hence to open up wide vistas into realms of hope and ambition.

The old thought led a person to "agonize" over their own sins and those of the world, hence to place much stress on repentance, reformation, and regeneration; the new holds that each person is already saved, is already potentially what they shall presently become in expression when they acknowledge their true birthright. The old called for strenuous methods of prayer and missionary work, while the new emphasizes the power of faith, silent

Exposition

expectancy, and mental attraction. According to the old we should acquire a new will, and this can come only as a gift of the Holy Spirit, the divine grace; but the new holds that "regeneration" is really a process of realizing or expressing our true self. The new refers to the inner center in each person as the region of all spiritual resources, the basis of power and life. At this center one may unite with infinite Life, Wisdom, Power. Here one may find guidance for every possible occasion. Consequently, it is not self-abnegation that is called for on our part, not resignation, and not sheer effort to meet the hardest incentives to moral discipline; but acceptance and expression of the true self.

The Starting Point. In order to appreciate the New Thought in this its fullness, we must put ourselves in the attitude of one who believes they have full right to turn directly to the highest spiritual sources, who acknowledges no authority save that of experience with its "leadings," and who finds in "ideal suggestion" a panacea for human ills. This attitude by no means implies lawless self-assertion, but the belief that humanity has long lived under authority, in ignorance of its divine birthright. The universe is accepted as a place of law and order, but for each it is said to be what their own consciousness makes it. To know life as it is, one must seek the sources of power for oneself, and become one's own minister and physician. The discovery of the inner point of view implies an awakening to consciousness of higher powers which may be put to practical use. Hence the evidences of the New Thought are not primarily of an argumentative character, but are matters of experience. To know that the new consciousness is efficient, you must test it by actual use, undertaking to verify through daily practice the truths which others have proved. That is, you should observe regular times for meditation, you should hold the most optimistic thoughts constantly before you, banishing all "negative" thoughts; and you should acquire the method of cure known as the silent or mental treatment.

The New Thought, unlike Christian Science, is not a body of doctrine which you are invited to accept before you receive treatment, but is a workable belief which you are asked to put to the test in all circumstances. This belief has grown out of successful experience, and has been made to cover the whole of life because it is said to have brought the desired results.

The implied beliefs are: the immediate or direct presence of God regarded as Spirit; the power of each person as a spirit to draw upon the divine presence; and the influence of deeply interior or spiritual states on mental life as a whole, hence on the body. God is thought of as the author of health, happiness, peace, freedom, success; not of their opposites. Hence the aim is, to put the soul or self into the best attitude to picture or conceive the divine ideal for each person, the ideal of health and freedom. The ideal thus dwelt upon in silent receptivity and concentration is forcefully impressed upon the mind, thence upon the deeper self or subconscious mind. The ideal or suggestion has power to eliminate adverse mental and physical conditions. For it is not simply a question of banishing conscious fears and wrong beliefs. It is not these alone that cause our illnesses and other troubles. Our whole mental storehouse must be cleansed. The entire mental life, conscious and subconscious, must become favorable.

The Test. It is not necessary to wait for trouble or

illness to try this method. The way to test it is to absent oneself from the multitude for a little while each day, put aside all thought of the busy world, and endeavor to be inwardly still. Some effort is required to turn away from the rush and hurry of the external world. One seems to be more apart of it than one realized. Time is required to let the usual activities, excitements, and other distracting states subside. Then one begins to discover what is needed by way of the elimination of nervous tension and excitability, the cultivation of inner repose and the development of powers of concentration and control.

It is not simply a question of relaxation or receptivity. Relaxation is essential, but might be overdone, might lead beyond mere restfulness to sleepiness and lassitude. Receptivity is a means rather than an end. Open-mindedness at random or in general is not ordinarily accompanied by good results. Nor is it desirable merely to "make the mind a blank." If one needs rest or sleep, it may be well to enjoy relaxation for a time. But spiritual meditation is an active process. Concentration is not vagueness or a mere yielding to the thought of the moment; it is definite focusing of consciousness on a desired end or ideal. Much depends upon the selection of an interest or idea worthy of contemplation. A definite clue can best be found by reading for a time in an uplifting essay or psalm, until the mind seizes upon an absorbing idea. One's progress will naturally depend upon the effort made to understand and overcome all obstacles to effective meditation. Much will also depend upon the philosophy one brings to the experience. Hence the importance of the New Thought as a view of the whole of life, based on an interpretation of the activities in process in our consciousness.

The test comes for most of us, therefore, when we break away from custom and begin to think for ourselves. Instead of looking to the far past for light we then regard the present moments of experience as most real. This emphasis on the pulsating life within us leads to the thought of God as "omnipresent wisdom," hence to the idea that present experience is in every way best for the immediate needs of the soul. Thus to accept and dwell on the present is not of course to become resigned to appearances, or reconciled to God's will, or stoically to acquiesce in life as given; but to enter in full adjustment into the life and the conditions just now being given by the quickening presence of God, the conditions called for by one's state of development, which is always in process. The clue is taken from life, from the vivifying process, not from crystallized creeds or established usages implying fixity and conservatism. The divine presence is regarded as dynamic. Vitalizing and dynamic, affirmative and expectant must be one's thought to be truly worthy and receptive. Each person as a spirit is primarily an active being, not a mere channel. Each person must move forward in order to be in adjustment with the Life that ever quickens and sustains them. Each of us must move forward to receive the guidance of the inner light.

Idealism. The implied philosophy is a species of idealism of the practical type. The first Reality is God thought of as Spirit, manifested in the entire universe of the spiritual order and in the natural world. To start with this Reality is to regard the spiritual or eternal world as intimately near, and as more real and enduring than the natural world of space and time. Here is the basis of all causality, all creative purposes.

Exposition

Here is the source of all efficient power. To the spiritual world external things are added as means of expression. Thus the human spirit is given a physical body as an agency of expression, and of response to the world. It does not follow that the visible world is a dream or illusion, but simply that it is secondary in value and reality, is without life or power of its own. Hence it is a question of assigning to their proper place the various things and forces that constitute the world. One need not enter into the subtleties of idealism as a philosophy. The main point lies in emphasis on the realities of the spirit, on the power of ideals. Everything depends upon the point of view, the look outward upon the world with the eyes of the spirit.

These matters will become clear if we note the way in which they were developed, that is, out of practical experience. As an idealistic belief this philosophy is indeed very old. So are many of the special tenets of the New Thought. But the re-discovery in our time of principles known long ago in ancient India and other lands came very gradually as the result of long and patient effort.

CHAPTER TWO

Historical Sketch

The American mental-healing movement was already well established when the term "New Thought" was first applied to it. It began in the United States with the investigations and therapeutic practice of Phineas Parkhurst Quimby (born 1803), of Belfast, Maine. It was not known to any extent outside of Maine until Quimby's death, in 1866, and the subsequent scattering of his followers and patients. Quimby was not a well-read man, and there was no healer or teacher for him to follow when he took up the new interest, nothing in short save a clue afforded by mesmerism, then somewhat in vogue. He knew little about the teachings of his age, and depended almost wholly upon his own experience and insights. Quimby did not even study the Bible in the light of mental healing until his experience gave him the incentive, and then he made his own interpretation, not that of any church.

As usual in the case of one who departs from accepted standards and breaks his way in fields untrodden in his generation, Quimby was misunderstood, particularly by those who identified his work with spiritualism, and by those who misrepresented him. Three lines of influence have come from his work and teaching, and without reference to these the healing movement cannot be explained. The misrepresentations have been due to an attempt to account for Christian Science as if, unlike all other teachings in the world, it sprang full-fledged into being by revelation without connection with human errors and quests for truth. But this is one line of influence simply, and does not concern us here. Another was due to the leadership of Quimby's most intimate followers. Elsewhere I have given an account of these leaders and their work. The third line of influence sprang from the writings and practice of Reverend Warren Felt Evans of Salisbury, Massachusetts, who received treatment from Quimby in Portland, in 1863, and was the first to carry the new interests outside of Maine.

Mr. Evans, who was formerly identified with the New Church, conversed with Quimby to exceptional advantage. He readily adopted Quimby's views, and interpreted them in accordance with the idealistic philosophy which he had acquired from Berkeley and others, and he also drew upon the writings of Emanuel Swedenborg. Mr. Evans published the first book on the general subject, *Mental Cure* in 1869, and for years he was the most influential author. His *Divine Law of Cure,* 1881, is still one of the best expositions of the underlying religious and philosophical principles. It was widely read by some of the earliest New Thought writers. The New Thought has, however,

Historical Sketch

become much more complex, different in tone, and wider in scope. Evans was much more widely informed than most New Thought writers, and his works abound in quotations from the philosophers whose teachings he identified with the theory of mental healing as he understood it. The New Thought writers, on the other hand, have kept more closely to practical experience as they viewed it. Hence they have not directly copied from Evans.

The First Misconception. In his reaction against the materialism of his day Mr. Quimby undoubtedly meant to establish a view of life founded on fact, spiritually interpreted. But many of his statements seemed to imply an idealistic view of matter similar to that attributed to Berkeley, as if the material world existed only in "idea." Hence his teachings were understood by some to mean denial of the substantial universe. Evans seized upon this aspect of Quimby's theory, and put an idealistic interpretation on the whole teaching. He thereby prepared the way for the one-sided doctrines of Christian Science and certain phases of the New Thought. Hence Mary Baker Eddy's claim that she "agreed with Berkeley," and her cardinal proposition: "All is mind; there is no matter." As usual in the case of most movements that gain a firm hold on popular thought, it was the least rational interpretations that became generally known. The world still waits for the kind of science Quimby had in mind. This science will not turn on the denial of facts, or the sheer assertion of "ideal suggestions," but will acknowledge and look far beyond natural facts to spiritual principles that include them. The wiser New Thought leaders have caught a glimpse of this science, and it would not be fair to judge them or their work by the popular doctrine here under consideration. It should also be remarked that Berkeley's idealism, misinterpreted, has been put to an illegitimate use by those who thought Berkeley denied the existence of the natural world.

Mr. Evans states that he was an idealist when he went to Mr. Quimby. "Reid's attempt to refute Berkeley," he says, "made me a convert to idealism more than two, score years ago." That is, Evans became an idealist before he became a devotee of Swedenborg. He took Swedenborg to be an idealist, and classed him, erroneously, with Hegel, Fichte, and Berkeley. Thus prejudging, Evans also took Quimby to be an idealist of Berkeley's type.

"Matter," Evans says, "is an unsubstantial appearance and is created and governed by thought." "[People] err when they suppose objects exist independent of a perceiving mind." From these conclusions concerning matter it was an easy step for Evans to proceed to the added conclusion that, "disease being in its root a wrong belief, change that belief, and we cure the disease." Mrs. Eddy reasoned in the same way when, having declared that "false sense evolves, in belief, a subjective state of mortal mind, which this same mind calls matter," she concluded that "disease is a false belief ... sickness is a delusion."

Now, it is not easy for the devotee of mental healing to correct this view without dropping back into the usual position, acknowledging the independent potency of matter, and weakly yielding to material circumstance. But somewhere between these extremes the truth lies. What needs to be remedied is not the notion that matter exists, for our beliefs never played the slightest part in creating it, but our attitude toward matter, particularly our own body. We need to become strong enough to admit all the facts of life, to accept the physical universe in all its strength and beauty as a divine product, and yet assign the human mind to its proper place.

The prime difficulty with the view adopted by Mr. Evans and Mrs. Eddy, and borrowed from them by hundreds of others, lies in its implied psychology. Briefly speaking, it is *a psychology without a body.* The body being dispensed with, the inference readily follows that mind can accomplish anything it will. Hence the door is open for any number of misconceptions. But the real point is to use the mind most effectively to master and purify the body. This cannot be accomplished save through genuine knowledge of the human mind in relation to the body. Such a view undermines the teachings of Mr. Evans and Mrs. Eddy concerning matter. Thus to look to psychology for aid is not necessarily to qualify the idealism of the New Thought, but to find a secure basis for rational suggestions, as we shall presently see.

The Later History. Passing by the beginnings of Christian Science, 1875-1882, we come to a time when the idealistic interpretations of Quimby's theory set on foot by the writings of Mr. Evans and Mrs. Eddy had gained sufficient hold in Boston so that readers and former students began to branch out for themselves. The "Mind Cure" or "Boston Craze," as it was first called, gradually spread to other cities, assuming new forms with each new leader. Thus a former student of Christian Science established the new movement in Hartford, Connecticut, and from that center teachers went to New York, where a variation of the mind-cure became known as "Metaphysical Healing." Gradually the movement spread to western cities, where it became known under yet other terms, such as "Practical Christianity," in Kansas City;[††] and "Divine Science" in San Francisco and Denver.

After 1890, a new school of writers appeared, among them Henry Wood and Ralph Waldo Trine, who gave a larger meaning to the original term, and endeavored to make of the "Thought" a comprehensive theory for the whole of life. A church was established in Boston as early as 1886, and since that time many Sunday meetings have flourished for brief periods. Magazines also began to appear early, and an active effort to spread the ideas began. A general convention was also held during that period, although it was many years before a national convention was undertaken. The first "Metaphysical Club" was organized in 1895. It was followed by similar clubs, "centers" and "circles" in various parts of the country. Presently[‡‡] the diversity of books and magazines became such that it was difficult even for close students of the movement to keep the run of them. Out of this diversity has come the New Thought as known today.

The New Thought in this its wider sense is indeed an expression of the liberalism of the age, a part of the "metaphysical movement" which followed New England transcendentalism. Thus, given the clue, one may trace connections between its tenets and those of the Unitarians. Again, the New Thought is an expression of the practical spirit of our age; it might be regarded as an aspect of pragmatism as advocated by William James. It would be possible, however, greatly to over-emphasize these relationships. Thus the New

---

[††] "Practical Christianity" became what is known today as Unity one of the largest branches of New Thought in the 21s century.
[‡‡] Dresser is writing in 1917.

Thought would appear to be merely general. The real cause of the movement, humanly speaking, was a definite need experienced by people who had turned from the churches. Whatever its later affiliations, this movement was due to the pioneer work of those who practiced healing. To know why and how it came to be we must put ourselves sympathetically in line with the original method of healing, and trace its development.

How Quimby Began. Mr. Quimby believed himself incurably diseased and likely at any time to die, when he began his investigations in the new field. Believing medical science to be a failure, he was ready to try any other method that might afford relief. It is this attitude of apparent hopelessness or self-abandonment which sometimes opens for us the door into a new world. Hence Mr. Quimby's willingness to adopt a wholly different point of view, the supposition that disease is not the sort of thing we take it to be, and people are not the kind of beings we think they are. Hence he was ready to experiment even with mesmerism for a time, and to make use of a "sensitive" or "subject."

Quimby's experiments with his "sensitive" soon showed him that a credulous person, accepting a physician's diagnosis, may believe they have a disease when in reality they are simply under a mental disturbance of a very different nature. Thus the apparent disease may seem more real to a sick person than an actual malady not apparent. To diagnose a patient mentally may be to discover what they think is their disease, trace its origin to some adverse opinion, and hence find the way to dispel it by explaining the nature and development of the imprisoning opinion. Mr. Quimby found that when a patient is thus freed from a haunting opinion, or misleading diagnosis, a quick cure is likely to follow, since the fears, tensions, and nervous excitements are associated with the adverse opinion and virtually constitute the disease. Having found out how his "subject" gained this information concerning a sick person's inner state, namely, through intuition and clairvoyance, and that others could acquire the powers by making the effort, Quimby no longer needed his "subject" as an intermediary. This was his turning point from mesmerism (hypnotism) to mental and spiritual healing. Moreover, this "subject" had diagnosed Quimby's own case and put such a different interpretation on the symptoms that Quimby, following the clue, regained his health and began to heal others by the same principle, not hypnotic but spiritual. The transition from the experimental to the later stage was made possible by Quimby's discovery concerning "the spiritual senses," as he called them -- that is, the power of intuitive discernment. The term "sense" was employed because the process of discernment sometimes included sight and feeling, the detection of mental atmospheres, as well as an intuition concerning character.

In contrast with a physician's diagnosis of disease based on the examination of symptoms, Mr. Quimby's starting-point was with the interior mental condition, conscious and subconscious. Quimby used the term "spiritual matter" to indicate that the subconscious is intermediate between mind and body. This included not merely the belief in the given disease, but a prevailing attitude towards disease as purely physical in origin, and various unconscious tendencies favorable to illness, suffering, and misery in general. It also included insight into the patient's disposition, their attitude towards life, and all the influences that shape life from within.

Seated receptively by the sick, and holding his mind open to mental impressions, also to spiritual guidance, Quimby found that he could not only discern the fears, disturbing emotions, haunting mental pictures, false beliefs, and the like, but substitute other mental states for those that caused the trouble. That is to say, a prevailing fear tended in one direction, towards ill-health, while an ideal of health and happiness tended in the other, aroused a new process favorable to recovery. The direction of mind once changed, the new mental imagery once established, the restorative process could be furthered by the "spiritual realization," as it would now be called, which Quimby carried on while sitting by the patient. This method grew under Quimby's hands and became an established mode of treatment. This method underlies the entire mental-healing movement and is what distinguishes it from hypnotism, faith-cure, and other forms of psychical treatment. It was acquired from Quimby by his patients, and developed in various ways according to the theory attached to it, as in the case of Evans and his extreme idealism. It grew under Quimby's hands because his experience fostered discernment, receptivity, and powers of concentration, together with ability to draw upon spiritual sources of healing-power; and because his practice with hundreds of cases gave Quimby more knowledge of mental influences and types of character. What was at first an experimental art thus became what he called a "science," a science because he knew how he performed his cures and could explain the principle to others.

Experience, not theory, was the guide. Experience opened a new field, and Quimby walked in it. The theory grew out of the practice. It led eventually to religion, hence to an interpretation of Christianity, partly because Quimby found that religious beliefs and emotions were partial causes of disease; and partly because the experience of sitting silently by the sick to heal them assumed a religious form. Thus in a natural sort of way Quimby not only gave people back their health but led them into practical forms of religion. Profoundly impressed by their restoration to health under spiritual auspices, it was not strange that Quimby's patients found in his teachings a substitute for former modes of belief and worship. They did not discard the Bible, but began to understand Christianity for the first time, and adopted the new practice of silent "realization." Thus each person began to experiment and verify for themselves.

The Central Principle. Quimby's mental starting-point is found in his statement that "whatever we believe, we create." This means that if we accept a diagnosis or opinion, the fear of death or hell, a dogma or creed as true, it is true for us, and generates its own mental world to which we attach ourselves. Quimby held that instead of sounding matters to the foundation, the majority of people judge by appearances and credulously enter into ill-founded beliefs. Thus under bondage to the verdicts of physicians concerning our health, the opinions of priests about the soul, and the influences of conventional society, we are not true to our real nature as spiritual beings. If we knew ourselves, we could take our troubles to the divine wisdom, ever present with us, and gain immediate help. For God meant us to be well, "disease is an invention of man," and every resource we could ask for is at hand.

Quimby therefore undertook to bring his patients to judgment; show them their bondage to errors and opinions, and a mistaken view of matter; and aid each one to turn to the divine sources for themselves. He cared nothing for the external symptoms of disease, but sought the inner causes, the repressed emotions, suppressed desires, misinterpreted feelings, and haunting mental pictures. His treatment, partly silent, partly conversational, was in tended, as he said, "to disabuse the mind of its errors," and establish the truth in their place. This truth included statements concerning the nature of each person as a spiritual being, the spiritual world, the spiritual life to which each person may become open intuitively, and the idea of God as ever-present wisdom. The truth in this sense of the word was, Quimby declared, "the cure," the revelation of each person's real situation in life. He did not claim his wisdom as his own, and took no credit to himself as a healer, but firmly believed in immediate divine guidance. It is well to bear this in mind, since it is on these points that some of the devotees of mental healing departed from its spiritual basis.

Quimby's teaching turned to such an extent on the contrast between opinion and wisdom, that later devotees, catching the original teaching in part, and influenced by Mr. Evans's idealism, made of the whole theory a "thought," to the neglect of the will and the emotions. Thus while Quimby regarded his own thought as an instrument of the divine wisdom, others a generation later declared thought to be "the greatest power in the world," characterizing it as unqualifiedly "creative" or "formative." Thus, too, it became a matter of custom to seek the causes of all diseases in "wrong thoughts" to the neglect of the emotions, attitudes, adverse nervous states, and bodily conditions favoring disease; while the process of cure was declared to be "right thinking." The prime result was the conclusion that "all causation is mental," a statement likely to turn the center of interest from divine or spiritual causality to human or mental causes.

Quimby did not originate these generalizations. These were due to Henry Wood and other New Thought writers who gave shape to the movement after 1890. Quimby would have pointed out that all true causality is divine, while each person's thought possesses a measure of power within the small world of their consciousness. It would thus be a question of discerning the deceptive thoughts and opinions, the "formative" mental pictures and the like through which in a purely relative way we create *for ourselves* what we believe. Looking deeper, Quimby sought through his intuition to find the true causes of life, and to establish the divine truth in place of the human thought. Hence he depended on insight and analysis rather than on "suggestion," since raised by mental therapists to the supreme place, sometimes to the exclusion of the idea of God.

Quimby indeed recognized the power of suggestion, under the guise of "error" or "opinion," but passed beyond it to wisdom. He held that the mind of each person is plastic, impressionable; it is like fertile soil. The lower or natural mind . . . the "carnal mind" of St. Paul, the "mortal mind" of Mary Baker Eddy . . . is indeed a sort of "spiritual matter" in which thoughts or opinions germinate. This would now be called "amenability to suggestion." It is not a desirable possession but a state to be understood and conquered that we may lift our consciousness so as to possess by contrast what St. Paul calls "the mind of the Spirit," the mind of Christ. In most of us it is a "subconscious mind," a phase of mental life of which we are unaware until we learn the influence and effect of mental atmospheres, mental contagions, and the like.

This amenability to suggestion is particularly true of the twilight region of our consciousness, into which fancies and fears enter with great ease. At the point where this mental twilight is lost in the darkness that envelops our mental processes and hides them from our sight the mind is profoundly susceptible. Here is where the greatest mischief is played. But here, too, is the responsive region which is made most of by the spiritual therapist. For our subconscious must be changed before the body will respond, and before the conscious self knows that the therapeutic process has begun. In this twilight region we are open to the illuminating presence of God. What we need is the light of the divine idea which shall disperse the darkness of error. A receptive patient is particularly open to such illuminations. The therapist is the friendly lamp-bearer who guides the way through the dark journeys of the soul.

The Power of Thought. See why an idea strikes home and produces subconscious results and you have the whole process in outline. For example, if someone makes a remark which gives rise to an initiatory emotion of anger on my part, and if hateful thoughts are thereby suggested so that I give way to the emotion and let it grow, it is plain that to harbor the thought of hatred is to find myself the victim of consequences which come as matters of course. The anger forthwith gains control, the blood rushes to my head, my cheeks become hot, I clinch my fists, and strike a blow. The results which ensue later . . . the headache, the remorse because of my indiscretion, the general nervous disturbance . . . are not the real trouble but its effects. The cause was the emotion or anger, hatred, animosity. The thought of anger grew upon me because I accepted it, permitted it to draw its like and increase. What I had power to control was the thought, the first emotion. Lacking in inner control, or failing to exercise my powers, I allowed my wrong thought to develop and grow until it became a harmful state of mind. I ought to have checked myself as soon as my mind turned in a harmful direction.

Likewise all troubles are said to grow out of minor causes because at the critical juncture we accept opinions, enter into errors, entertain unfortunate thoughts. The wrong direction of mind gives shape to the subconscious, and the involuntary organism accomplishes the rest. Likewise the cure involves a changed direction of mind, a sentiment of peace in place of discord, a spirit of forgiveness where there was condemnation, an attitude of love instead of hatred. When I turn from hatred to love, from excitement to peace, my general consciousness responds, the excitement subsides, a subconscious change follows, and the organism does its part correspondingly. Everybody knows he has power to change from hatred to love. We all know more or less about the consequences of jealousy, worry, nervous wear and tear, and emotional excitement of various kinds. We know too that our lusts and appetites eat into our substance. We are well aware that the general mode of life has much to do with the diseases which

Historical Sketch

grow out of our conduct. Make the most of this, learn much more in the same direction, and you will have the beginnings of mental healing. Go further still, trace these disturbing emotions and thoughts to selfishness, and your theory will become spiritual, for you will realize that a change of heart will be needed to establish a complete cure. Thus the therapeutic interest passes gradually into the larger field of the spiritual life.

CHAPTER THREE

The Silent Method

Mental treatment is devised to reach the subconscious states of which the patient is ignorant. In nearly every case the healer finds that fear and nervousness have been important factors. Naturally the healer makes much use of "realizations" tending to allay fear and calm the nervous states. If the treatment removes the fears, haunting mental pictures, and other adverse mental states; if it takes away the nervous tension and quiets the nervous whirlwinds, the bodily responses will accomplish the rest in nature's own way. The central point is an elevating thought, a word of peace or faith which gives definiteness to the spiritual realization; as you might say to yourself, "Be still," when tempted to yield to anger. The reiteration of the decisive word is necessary in order to make the requisite impression. Thus the New Thought method of "entering the silence" by employing idealistic affirmations has had a natural history. This method is now employed for general purposes in place of prayer, because it was found efficient in treating the sick. The affirmations are of an ideal character because the effort is to establish trust in the place of fear, love instead of hate. The central thought is believed to be "formative," because through the subconscious it draws corresponding conditions. The affirmation, impressed upon the subconscious, establishes a new center of equilibrium, precisely as the sentiment of peace drives out the thought of anger. The conditions of receptivity and expectant attention are necessary in order that the desired impression may be made.

Thought and Will. This principle will become clearer if we note that it is not the one on which the ancient Hebrews placed stress. The Hebrews were impressed by the consciousness of sin, the alienation from Jehovah through wrong acts of will. Regeneration was to come about, so far as human initiative could secure it, through obedience, through readjustment of the will. According to the New Thought the trouble with humanity is not primarily sin or evil; this is why the resource is not found in moral regeneration of the will. The trouble is said to lie in human ignorance, error; the will is seldom mentioned. People are plainly ignorant of the truth that they are spiritual beings having power over their organism in health and disease. People unwittingly associate harmful ideas with sensations and inner states of various sorts, and thereby creates their own misery. They fall into numberless misconceptions in regard to their situation in life, hence becoming a victim of their own opinions. By long association people have connected various aches and pains with certain names, so that whenever one feels the pain one assumes that they have caught the disease signified by the name. In the same way certain effects are associated with liquids and

The Silent Method

powders, until these, used as medicines, actually produce the results which the habitual thought has associated with them. Many other substances besides poisons have likewise acquired apparent qualities of their own. Freedom from all these unfortunate associations comes through the discovery that "wrong thought" is the potent factor. The same power that has brought us our misery will bring us happiness and health when new thoughts establish new associations. It is "the truth" which sets people free. Consequently, the prime requisite is not a doctrine of sin, a scheme of salvation, a plan for the training of the will; it is knowledge of the types of consciousness which create misery and suffering, and of the sorts of affirmation which dispel wrong beliefs, banish fears and other disturbing emotions.

This point of view is so unusual that we must approach it in a number of ways to make sure that we understand it. Ordinarily, one distinguishes between people's active powers and their thoughts. Psychologically speaking, thought is not creative in a volitional sense, but its function is to imitate or represent; while the will makes the decisions and acts upon the acceptable idea. Consequently, we would maintain that one might "hold good thoughts" for ever, and make little headway, since a thought or mental image is not ordinarily supposed to have formative power. But in the New Thought no such distinction is made. Thought is regarded as practically synonymous with action. What we believe we act upon. What we believe or think at heart, what we hold in mind, forthwith gives form to our inmost attitude, so that we "attract" corresponding conditions. A person's physical condition corresponds to their prevailing thoughts. If you see someone bowed down and limping with rheumatism, you may know that they have held angry, contracting, selfish thoughts. If poor and/or miserably placed in life, you may infer that they are lacking in confidence, a victim of fear and mental weakness. To cure them you must bring them in to a state of buoyant belief in themselves in which they hold up their heads in confidence. Carry this process far enough, and it will be found to cover the whole of life. It will not then be necessary to speak of sin or evil; freedom comes through right thinking, the decisive power is in our hands.

Thought and Reality. An illustration will make this point clear. If you and I should enter a forest at night, we might readily create in imagination many a fearful shape out of harmless stumps and rocks. If we were denizens of a superstitious age, these figments of the imagination would become realities for us, and we should dwell in a world of our own fancy. The resource in such a case would be to examine each of the dark objects around us in the forest, discover the actual facts, and thereby disabuse the mind of its errors. We should then judge, not by the appearance, but by what we knew to be the truth concerning the rocks and trees. In a similar way we might examine our beliefs, distinguishing between the experiences we actually feel and the emotions or ideas associated with them. Thus we might examine and understand all things in life, if we possessed the right clue. Life for most of us is an ill-defined wandering amidst circumstances which we do not understand. Born in ignorance, we mistake our bodies for ourselves, and enter into bondages without limit, deeming ourselves creatures of mere things, climate, weather. If we knew our true estate, we should know that as children of God we are gifted with superior powers which we seldom use. Our struggles and woes are explicable by the fact that, like people in a forest mistaking stumps for wild beasts, we make of life what we put into it, and become victims of our fears. If you are in an ill-natured, disconsolate frame of mind, your world will correspond. If happy, optimistic, ready to make the utmost of every opportunity, you will find the world like your prevailing state of mind. The trouble is not in the world; it is in you. Mend your mood, and you shall mend your world.

The real trouble is never physical, and cannot be cured by physical means. The physiological conditions really exist, to be sure; and when someone believes they have a headache or the rheumatism, they really have it. But the external appearances are like the imaginary forms seen in the dark forest. The physician has made a mistake in diagnosing the bodily symptoms, noting the temperature, inquiring about the sleep or the digestion. All causes are mental; and to know why someone has heart disease or rheumatism, you must know what sort of consciousness they have put into their life; you must examine their beliefs and fears.

The Origin of Disease. Take a more specific instance. Someone feels a slightly painful sensation about the heart; and having heard of heart disease, readily misinterprets the sensation and concludes that they are already a victim. To attach a name to a sensation is to add to its power; and the name "heart-disease" is especially potent. Stirred by increasing fears, this person hurriedly consults a physician, describes the pain, and is assured that they really have the dreaded disease. This verdict adds to the power of the idea, and the person's mind now becomes filled with the wrong consciousness which the idea generates. The idea takes hold of the person's subconscious, affects the nervous system, throws the organism more out of adjustment, and gradually creates conditions corresponding to it, until the person really has heart disease, and is likely to be seized by the arch-fear, death. This is one of Quimby's explanations of the cause of disease.

Now, if instead of being treated as a physician would treat the case, this person is put under the care of a mental healer, the procedure would be somewhat as follows. The therapist is supposed to be one who sees not only the illusions of the stumps and the rocks, but the real rocks and trees in the forest. In this case the rocks and trees represent the person's spiritual welfare as God conceivably regards it. That is, God meant us to be well, and we always are well in reality. Sickness, Mr. Quimby declared, is an error or "invention," due to misinterpretation of aches and pains. If the person in question had turned in consciousness to God, when they felt the first tinge of pain, affirming and realizing their oneness with God, the pain would have ceased, and a normal state of consciousness would have driven out the fear. The disease was "created" by wrong thought out of a sensation which was misunderstood. The person is still ignorant of all this, hence must be helped by the mental therapist until they can personally realize the renewing presence of God. God beholds each person in their integrity as God's child, free, sound, sane. The therapist's part is to establish in the person's consciousness this divine image, so that the person may be freed from error, and restored to their true estate as a spiritual being.

The Method of Realization. In our supposed forest, you might discover ahead of me that the bear

The Silent Method

we were afraid of was only a stump. If I doubted, you would bid me draw near and look, assuring me that there was nothing to fear. Finally you would lead me to the stump to prove that you were right. What you would be telling me about the stump would correspond to the realization or affirmation of the healer who aims to banish from the person's mind the notion that they have heart-disease. That is, the healer, sitting in silence by the patient, would put their mind through a process somewhat as follows, addressing their thought to the patient's inmost self:

"Peace be with you. I come as a messenger of peace to bring freedom and happiness. Let us realize the peace and goodness of God. You are God's child, perfect in ideal, strong, well, and free. In God there is perfect peace and harmony, no discord at all. Let your fears and doubts go, that you may know God's peace and love. There is nothing to fear. Now your fears are going, you are becoming restful, trustful, and free. You are settling down, down into quietness and repose; the disturbance is subsiding; the tension is lessening. Now God's perfect ideal is being realized. You are at peace; you are well; you are healed."

This general realization, reiterated and made emphatic, would be followed by a more specific series of affirmations with reference to the particular need of the patient; and the disturbed region would be pictured in ideal terms in accordance with the standard of perfect health. This realization would be said to take effect in the organism of the patient through impressions produced on their subconscious. These impressions would, in turn, be regarded as producible because of the intimate relationship established between one 'mind and the other through receptivity and co-operative response, through mutual relationship with the divine presence. The silent realization would not, strictly speaking, be the same as a prayer; for God would not be called upon or addressed as in the act of worship. The assumption would be, that whatever is needed by this patient, they already in deepest reality possess; they are healed now; in spirit they are at peace, they are already God's child, sound and sane in the divine image. The realization is intended to bring this truth into actuality, thereby dispersing the shadows and clearing away the errors. Whatever wisdom or power may be required to accomplish this result is at hand, and need not be asked for in prayer; the healer's part is to enter into the divine life already at hand, and become an agent for it. The essence of this method lies in the fact that the treatment or realization is a concrete way of making spiritual truth real and vivid. Devotees of it sincerely believe that they have found a way to make Christianity practical. They do not claim that their fundamental principles are new. The novelty or originality is said to lie in the method.

Thus we see why the mental therapist follows an inner clue, virtually ignoring the traditional conceptions of disease and its cure. The inner clue is followed in accordance with the healer's clairvoyant or intuitive diagnosis. It implies the conviction that human life is really an affair of consciousness, a series of spiritual states, while our physical experience is an expression of these states. For example, Henry Wood says:

"The body is a grand composite photograph of previous thinking and mental states . . . Each person's physical organism, like that of all animate creatures, is built *by* its invisible resident, and not for them. Life expresses itself through matter, but this process is never reversed . . . The physical organism of each person manifests its own erroneous and false thinking of the past, and also, in some degree, that of humanity in general. (from *Ideal Suggestion through Mental Photograph by Henry Wood, 1899*, pp. 34, 80, 100)

From this point of view, we are like people witnessing a play dealing with the issues of modern life. Each of us maintains a certain conviction, or prevailing attitude. We get out of the play what we carry to it, permitting ourselves to be disturbed, or remaining outside of the excitement, according to the consciousness we bring. If we change our consciousness, we change the play. Life is indeed no play; it is real and earnest, but it was meant to be joyous and healthful. There are resources enough for us all. Every person was meant to stand upright and enjoy their own privileges. "The divine opulence is for all." It is the soul that makes circumstance, not circumstance that shapes the soul. To succeed you must first of all *believe* in success. Assume a courageous attitude, and you will find the world coming round to your position; new opportunities will reveal themselves, and everybody will help you to your goal.

Thus it comes about that great emphasis is put upon inner quietude, poise, receptivity, since these states attract the most desirable conditions. Thus the New Thought people affirm that they already are what they will to be; they already possess what they need. Their part is to be open, and responsive. By the same principle, one may "realize" for another in all the conditions of life, sending out good and loving thoughts. Nay further, our whole consciousness in daily life should conform to the ideals which we affirm in silence. We should think no ill, feel no resentment, enmity, or dislike; we should carry atmospheres of peace, love, and charity wherever we go, thinking the best about everybody, looking for the good in people, calling it forth, holding fast to it.

Spiritually interpreted, this teaching means that each person is directly open to the wisdom and power of God. The affirmation "God is here," is a favorite among New Thought people. To affirm that God is vitally present is to put the mind into an attitude to ascend to a higher level of consciousness. The Power thus apprehended is the real therapeutic agency. It is this Power that enters the soul of the healer and is thence transmitted to the subconscious of the patient, or directly received by the patient if open to it. Hence the healer does not claim to influence or control the patient's mind as in the case of hypnotism, but to be a channel of communication for spiritual life. (The silent treatment is radically different from all methods employed by hypnotists because the patient is not under hypnosis, but is merely receptive, and is encouraged to strengthen their own will, not to yield it to another.)

Jesus and Christ. As an agent of this life, one who is able to heal through right affirmation, the healer believes they are able to turn to God without mediator. That is, Christ for the New Thought is not a person, but a universal spiritual possibility -- the "Christ within" of every person who claims their oneness with God; while the man Jesus was the prophet of this consciousness. What Jesus did as a prophet or forerunner, you and I could do if we could as fully realize our oneness with God. He showed his consciousness by His works of healing. The Christian churches have lost sight of this practical phase of the

Christian life. In our time the therapeutic power has been rediscovered and put within the reach of all.

The distinction above implied is the basis of the teaching which in radical form is known as "Christian Science." Mr. Quimby developed his views without reference to Christian teaching -- that is, on a psychological basis, until he began to see the implied laws of cure. Then he turned to the Gospels with what seemed to him an illuminating clue. The works of healing attributed to Jesus were not, he concluded, miracles or wonders, due to infractions of law; but were accomplished through the application of principles perfectly understood by Jesus. These principles Jesus taught as a science, and this science was divine; it was the Christ-science or universal spiritual wisdom. The theological world has failed, in its deification of Jesus, to grasp the true science which Jesus taught. God indeed spoke through Jesus in those passages in which universal principles are enunciated, and the "Christ," or wisdom, thus speaking *was God.* But if we really understand the Christ we shall differentiate the universal from the personal, the man of flesh and blood, endeavoring to live by the Christ-science in daily conduct, and to prove it as a therapeutic principle.

Mr. Quimby believed that he had rediscovered this "science of life and happiness," this "Christian" science in contrast with medical science. Many of his articles are devoted to this distinction between the divine wisdom and the human selfhood. It was this "science" which Quimby imparted to Mary Baker Eddy, Warren Felt Evans, and others who interpreted it in their own manner. It would be unfair to attribute these varying interpretations to Mr. Quimby, but also unjust not to trace to him the original impetus.

The Interpretation of Scripture. The custom of interpreting the Bible in accordance with mental-healing principles also began with Quimby. Many of his manuscripts are devoted to these efforts to bring out the inner or spiritual meaning of the Bible. From Quimby the custom passed to Mrs. Eddy and thence to the New Thought in general. As a result, we have so many variations and often such fanciful interpretations that the reader of works on mental healing is bewildered. When Scripture is said to mean so many things, it hardly means anything at all. The resource would be to take the most thoroughgoing of these interpretations and make a careful study of the Scriptures from the implied point of view. It was Emanuel Swedenborg who set the example in this field by bringing forward the teaching that the series of books known as "the Word," in contrast with the Bible as a whole, contains a consistent inner meaning discoverable from Genesis to Revelation. Such a proposition is of course demonstrable apart from all personal interpretations and special applications. For it implies a theory of correspondence between the spirit and the letter which may be tested word by word, and chapter by chapter. Quimby caught enough of this method to apply it to the reading of the Bible in the light of his own illuminations, but did not undertake a study of the Scriptures in general. The important point for our purposes is the fact that followers of the New Thought have come to believe that the Scriptures contain a spiritual science.

The New Thought and Pantheism. With some of the later devotees of the New Thought the idea of "the Christ within," the "God-consciousness," has tended towards mysticism. That is, God has been identified with the soul, each person has been called "divine."

Thus a bond of connection has appeared with the spiritual pantheism of India, and the Hindu teachers of the Vedanta philosophy who began to come to the United States as a result of the World's Parliament of Religions in Chicago, in 1893. The main principle of this philosophy is that in reality there is but one Self (Atman) or Being (Brahman), while the various finite selves and the world are appearances due to separateness which may be overcome through spiritual contemplation and superconsciousness.

The crucial question would be, Does this spiritual pantheism afford the best explanation of the inner life, its practical needs and interests? Is nature an illusory world apparently existing in space and time but in fact due to our own ignorant, separated consciousness? Before adopting this philosophy it would be well to push Western individualism through to the end to see if it offers a more satisfactory explanation.

The New Thought is not necessarily mystical or pantheistic. It is more properly a form of individualism. The self that is affirmed as "divine" is the individual soul, not the infinite. The self affirms its "oneness" with God in order to separate the ideal self from the imprisoned self -- that is, for practical purposes. Ralph Waldo Emerson's teaching concerning the "Over-soul" might be taken as the clue in this connection. Some of Emerson's sentences come very near the proposition that "All is God," and his poem *Brahma,* is explicit pantheism. But, on the whole, Emerson is an individualist, the greatest prophet of "self-reliance." It is in this sense that the New Thought can best emphasize the potentialities of the individual.

Theosophy. There are also points of contact between the New Thought and Theosophy, and some of the leaders have incorporated theosophical principles into their teaching. For those who are interested in a highly developed theory of the several "planes" and "auras" Theosophy affords a fascinating field. One might adopt the methods of mental healing and practice them on a theosophical basis. The question would be whether the doctrine of reincarnation affords the best plan for the emancipation of the individual. Theosophy is surely right in its firm emphasis on the law of action and reaction. Here it harmonizes with the New Thought. But some of us are led to look at the question of salvation at very close range, instead of holding that we are loaded with the accumulated deeds (Karma) of past existences, or accepting the theosophical motive for avoiding further re-births. Practically speaking, we may be sure that we are building up a future which will correspond with the prevailing love of the soul. Most of people in the Western world would prefer to deal with the experiences that are close at hand, actuated by the motive of service, and seeking emancipation through service, leaving the issues of pre-existence and future existence open.

Spiritualism. Again, devotees of the New Thought have become allied with spiritism in its various forms. The prime difficulty with us in our divided selfhood and more serious illnesses, so some would say, is that we are reinforced by obsessing spirits. The resource would be to become aware of the tormenting spirit, break the connection, and cast the spirit out. In this process we might be aided by advanced spirits coo-operating with our therapeutic realizations. Thus we might adopt a spiritualistic interpretation of the entire mental-healing process. We might then regard the healer as a medium, the mental activity as merely incidental, the efficiency being due to the power of the advanced spirit operating through the organism of the healer. Thus the whole world of modern spiritualism would be opened up, and we would have many psychical problems to solve. We would then apparently have a satisfactory way to account for the cases of obsession recorded in the New Testament. The tendency would be to explain as many matters as possible on the supposition that spirits are continually acting upon or through us.

The tendency of thought in our age, however, is to adopt psychological explanations of matters near at hand. Thus Dr. Elwood Worcester and his collaborators in the textbooks of the Emmanuel Movement, such as *Religion and Medicine: The Moral Control of Nervous Disorders (1908),* have offered admirable psychological descriptions of the cases of obsession mentioned in the New Testament. Whatever the truth in the theory of obsession by spirits outside of the divided personality of the sufferer, what we have directly to deal with is the psycho-physical condition of the patient. If there be a connection with spirits the connection must be broken by removing its basis in the patient. This would have to be done in any event. The problem is simplified, therefore, if we deal directly with the psycho-physical condition and postpone to its proper time the problems of mediumship and other matters now treated under the head of psychical research. Moreover, individuals who are ready to face these matters in themselves must have a system of fundamental principles concerning the Holy Spirit before they can adequately deal with the relationship of disembodied finite spirits.

If one were to make a thorough study of all psychical influences before undertaking to resolve the crucial matters of the regenerating life, one would naturally turn to Swedenborg whose experience in relation to the world of spirits are said to have been more exhaustive than those of anyone else who has lived on this earth. Meanwhile, for most of us there is the immediate problem. Whatever we may say of hells organized in minute detail to provide for every type of person who prefers hell to heaven as a future abode, it is already clear that hell is self-will, self-love; while temptations and devils are the forces of the "old Adam" dying within us. Hell will cease for me in so far as, coming to judgment, facing my prevailing love, I alter my course and walk in life's divine pathway. I must do this eventually, whether I am a Theosophist, Spiritualist, or what not. If I realize that I am tempted because the Holy Spirit is leading me out of the clutches of the "old Adam," I need not be disconcerted any longer, but may wholly trust the guiding hand. However much the resistances of my lower nature may be reinforced from without, the Spirit is able to complete the process of regeneration. I am already in heaven in part if at peace with regard to the conditions through which I am progressing. For the true heaven for me is the sphere of work God has given me to do.

In other words, each of us is spiritually speaking where they belong, and each is being compensated according to their real achievement. With each change of heart there will be a corresponding change with regard to all that relates to the heart. For there is nothing in heaven or on earth to prevent the operation of the moral recompenses of the world. This is the ideal world. There could be none better.

The Law of Attraction. The whole question of correspondence between the inner and outer conditions is brought out into the clear light by considering the law of attraction, that is, by first noting what is within each person's power. It is within each person's power, for example, to control their impulses and emotions, to overcome inner friction, rebellion, complaint; and to eliminate all activities that impede or prevent mental efficiency. It is within each person's power to grow in philosophical knowledge, hence to learn the nature of the forces to which daily life must be adjusted. It is within each person's power to attach their consciousness to high ideals, growing steadily like them. One's power in all these directions lies especially *in the beginning of action,* rather than in the mere processes, habits, and functions which realize these beginnings. Consequently, the more control I have at the center the more I can accomplish. Each moment of my consciousness I have the power to rebel, reject, yield, or co-operate, according to my attitude, my way of meeting life. Thus while I am powerless by taking thought to change the order and method of the cosmos in any respect whatever, I can by taking my opportunities present a different front to the world. Hence I shall find myself drawn to changed conditions, as time passes. Hence I shall attract different conditions through the triumphs I win over those just now at hand.

I am not, therefore, like a ball cast about by the winds, or a piece of metal attracted by a magnet. The response elicited from me by the passing event seems indeed to have been called out by the event, as if I were a mere reacting instrument. Externally regarded I am a creature of circumstance. From the point of the brain I am a creature of habit. From the psychological point of view I am the product of my passing mental states. In a certain social light I appear to be the victim of "economic determinism." For in all these and other respects I am indeed "under the law," "bound to the wheel of life," as the Buddhists say. But in all these respects there is more to be said, in behalf of the inner life.

Each time I understand a force or law and conform to it in its proper place I am set free, as when the burnt child avoids the fire. The law of nature does not hold me down as it does the rock, worn away by inches through the action of wind and tide; but I am held down to the progressive discovery that I am a moral being, led on from opportunity to opportunity until I know myself. The law teaches me to obey, but when I conform I feel no constraint. If it seems a hardship that I must steadily meet life, living out to the end in my own fashion, instead of shirking responsibility, all this will surely be changed in my eyes when I awaken to the opportunities within my power, the joys and freedom which await me. What I need then, whether I adopt Theosophy or Spiritualism, the Vedanta philosophy or any other system meeting the New Thought at certain points, is a method by which to *realize my present state today,* by which to come to judgment. Hence the New Thought aims to be more practical, to apply the silent method to the needs of the hour.

Spiritual Meditation. We noticed above that the silent method of treatment developed out of Quimby's teaching that the causes of disease are in the mental world, and that there must be a way of effacing harmful mental pictures and other adverse impressions. By a further development in the same direction, the method of silence has come not only to take the place of prayer but of other forms of-worship; hence it has led to a revival of the old-time practice of the presence of God, and the Eastern custom of spiritual meditation. Unlike the mystics who in pious seclusion meditated on the divine presence, these modern devotees of silence gather in groups and meditate for practical purposes. They are not ascetics or hermits, but take the world as they find it. They do not regard nature as an "illusion," but endeavor to disengage their thoughts from the bondages of the flesh. Nor are they subject to the mystic ecstasy or beatific vision, the all-absorbing "cosmic consciousness" which came to some of the mystics of old. The objection to such ecstasy is that it may come only three or four times in a lifetime, or may breed an excessive emotional reaction; whereas "the silence" as now practiced may be regained at will, at any time, and is for practical purposes solely. It is customary in fact to take a single idea and concentrate upon it for fifteen minutes or so. Such an "ideal suggestion" as this, "The Spirit of God fills and thrills every atom of my being," may thus be the central point of the "realization." Some of the New Thought leaders send out each week or month such a statement as the following, to be used regularly during the appointed time: "I am Intelligence, and absorb the Life-giving Spiritualizing ray of God's Sunshine of Wisdom and Love."

Here are the directions for "entering the silence" given in the *Self-Culture Journal:*

"1. Retire every day to a quiet room alone, detaching yourself from everyone and everything for half an hour or longer if possible. Be alone with God in the Silence. 2. Take up a restful position, relax all your physical body and breathe deeply and rapidly for a few minutes. 3. Shut out all your daily thoughts and cares, allow none of the anxieties that harass you to occupy your mind. Let the door be barred against all sensation and bodily, mental or moral imperfections. See yourself perfect as the child of God. 4. When you are calm and peaceful take the following affirmations into your mind and hold them there to the exclusion of all others, and concentrate upon them. Give yourself up to it [the given affirmation] and endeavor to realize what it means to you. 5. Let the affirmation fill you, until gradually a sweet rest and peace steals over you, and you will feel the Infinite Life vibrating through you, until life, strength, and love overflow your entire being. Use the thought every day to ensure success, for this is a daily growth into Wholeness. Let no discouragement or fear have place in your mentality. *You must grow.* Thoughts or affirmations for meditation: Oh God, Thy Perfect Health is revealed in me. Thy Infinite Power upholds me. Thy Almighty Strength is my support. Thy Unchanging Love surrounds me. Thy Infinite Wisdom guides me. Thy Wondrous Intelligence illumines my mind."

The Prosperity Treatment. By a further extension of the same method the cardinal idea of mental healing has more recently been applied to the conditions that pertain to success.

"Genuine prosperity," says one New Thought writer, for example, "is fundamentally a matter of consciousness, and when this fact is recognized and properly understood the individual is well on the way to manifesting it objectively, whatever the outward appearances may be temporarily. The psychological principles involved in manifesting physical health, social success, financial success, and general harmony are so similar that the true realization of them in one direction will inevitably assist the student in all directions."

If then our illnesses are chiefly due to wrong attitudes, beliefs, fears, and other adverse mental states, our failures in business and in life generally must be due to the same causes. If a weak, negative attitude "attracts" mental and other conditions corresponding with it, an affirmative attitude will draw its like. Thus when one becomes affirmative with regard to the conditions that make for sound health, one naturally applies the same set of expectations to all other desirable phases of life. If a patient may be successfully treated for disease by the mental method, they may also be treated for prosperity, or may secure prosperity for themselves by employing the right ideal suggestion. Poverty has in fact been called a "disease " -- that is, an adverse mental state. Wealth must then be primarily a mental possession. We obtain wealth if our attitude invites it, if we deny the possibility of poverty.

Coming to Judgment. This method seems attractive indeed, so the critic will say, to those born under favorable conditions, but what of people who were born in the slums, of ignorant parents, deficient in capacity, held down to sheer labor in an uncongenial occupation? Is " the law of attraction" fair in such cases?

The reply is that we are all for spiritual reasons under the conditions that are right for us. If we still complain of the basis on which the world is organized, we have not yet come to judgment to understand the law in our own case. When we accept the conditions which life affords, we will find how true it is that "human nature is the same the world over." The same power that touches our heart, transforming us from unquickened beings into beings of love, is able to touch the heart of the worst criminal who ever lived.

The testimony of those who know is that when the most low-lived creature is rescued from a life of degradation the response is more immediate, the result more wide-reaching than in the case of converted souls in the ordinary walks of life. For the lowest sinner may possess greater openness to life, greater power to sin, in the first place, and greater power of self-abandonment when the call to a good life is sounded in the soul. Follow these lives still more closely, and you will find that what touches them is not a mere change in external conditions, when they are properly clothed and fed, given respectable occupations, or aided in their fierce struggle to overcome the desire for alcohol; it is a word of sympathy that opens the door of hope, an expression of love that rouses the soul, or an inward voice calling them to a changed life. What touches them is the manifestation of love which reaches them precisely where they are.

What affects one atom affects all. How much more true is this in the human world with the great power for upliftment that is granted those who profoundly repent. The more deeply the heart is touched the greater the power that goes forth from it. The same cosmos which seemed so cruel that it allows the miserable wretch born in the slums to go on for years a victim of poverty, drink, and, criminality, proves to be a world of love and righteousness when the great change takes place. Somehow this old world of ours has room for an enormous range from the most despicable sinner to the noblest saint. What rules it in the last analysis is plainly not the justice that is meted out in the courts, not the judgment of those who estimate people by material standards, but the great moral law which owns and guards us all -- the law that measures people by what they are at heart, by their present need, and by their welfare in the long run.

Compensation. In vain do we try to make this out to be a just world so long as we undertake to explain it from without. It is a world of the Spirit, of ideals, moral opportunities, and conquests. It becomes an order, a home of beauty, of goodness and joy, in so far as the observer is one consistent person in character, in attitude, in soul. The compensations of the real cosmos are often very unlike those which we demand, just as the punishment put upon us by our consciences differs from that decreed by the courts. But once accustom yourself to the moral point of view, and the revelation of the world's inherent goodness will dawn upon you. If you do not believe that honesty and fidelity, charity and love, win their reward, it is because you have not given them half a trial.

It is indeed true that the majority of people are engaged in getting all they can out of people with the least expenditure. It is indeed true that human nature is selfish, passionate, engaged in the process of emerging from animality into the first stages of humanity, occasionally dropping far below the level of the brute. We must acknowledge that people are where they are. But meanwhile the principle of giving is at work in the world. Turn from getting to giving and you will have little time for reflection on the selfishness of human nature, so absorbed will you be in the opportunities of the hour. The most deeply impressive consideration of all is the fact that we have the power to discern what the misguided person before us is capable of being. When I so far banish the world's standards as to extend the hand of welcome and utter the word of love to the one whom society would condemn, then indeed is this mundane realm made a paradise for me. Whenever, on the contrary, you hear me uttering complaints you may know that I am not meeting my opportunity.

The decisive center is not in our beliefs but in our character, the dynamic center which really attracts like conditions to us. If like a person I meet the opportunity that is given me, the first will lead to a second. My optimism must have backbone, must be moral to be efficient. Moreover, the activities that center in my character include the old as well as the new phases of my selfhood, for the law of attraction applies to the whole individual. Hence to make sure that my ideals shall be realized I must make them dynamic through conduct in their behalf, by seeing that the balance of power is established in their favor, as opposed to the resistances of my old selfhood.

If then I would grow in adaptation to this splendid world, let me begin by presenting a better combination of traits of character and moral deeds to serve as a new center of attraction. For my rational optimism bids me look to myself that wiser reactions may issue from me. When I know all the points of contact that involve me in undesirable experiences, I may rise above and transform them. Thus looking to myself I shall find little time for condemnation. But, looking to myself profoundly, I shall soon conclude afresh that even self-improvement is incomplete if it become an end in itself. For I am a social being, and when I really remedy my attitude I shall be prompted to summon the best from my associates.

Summary. The New Thought neither makes nor mars its followers. These carry into their new mental world whatever is in them. The best adopt the new belief reverently, and see in it a new revelation of practical Christianity; others make little or much of it

The Silent Method

according to their type. Thus it varies without limit according to the individual, despite the fact that the original teaching started out to become a " science." When the "Thought" became widely popular, there were some who saw in it a means to private ends, and made of it a mental rather than a spiritual teaching. Mr. Quimby's view was that the divine wisdom is the real efficiency, not our human thought; hence it is God, not a person, who heals. Quimby sought to bring his patients to judgment spiritually that they might know their actual standing. This teaching has sometimes been overlooked in the effort to affirm the importance of the human individual.

Granted the belief that each person may go to the supreme sources of wisdom and power, you would naturally expect that each would put their own interpretation upon the resulting experience. In a large-minded person this fidelity becomes a form of worship, leading to service. In a self-seeking person it becomes a new form of self-aggrandizement. To know the inmost spirit of the movement and understand why it has spread so widely, you must always suppose yourself in the position of one who is dissatisfied with medical practice and with the churches; and who sets out on an independent quest for health, happiness, and spiritual truth. The investigator finds satisfaction and peace because in the therapeutic realization of the presence of God one finds a ready resource in times of trouble. The "Thought" grows out of the experience, not the experience out of the doctrine. The experience comes to many with the force of a revelation, since it makes known for the first time the idea of the divine presence as the great resource to be drawn upon in every possible need. The inner clue once found, it is seen that health, happiness, prosperity, and the rest depend on our attitude toward life. The individual mind, then, is the attracting center. The essence of mind is thought, creative or affirmative thought. To see the nature and place of such thought is to be able to work out a complete point of view, hence to discover the true sources of religion and of all successful life.

CHAPTER FOUR

Estimate

It is plain from the history of the New Thought that the mental-healing doctrine has been in constant process of change since the various lines of interpretation branched off from the original teaching. The process is still going on. Under these conditions it might seem impossible to estimate the theory as a whole. The devotee is likely to prefer the interpretation put upon the movement by the particular group to which they belong. The outsider is likely to fail as critic because unable to appreciate the movement from within. Meanwhile, the New Thought, like Christian Science, has impressed our age; and one finds traces of its influence among people of liberal religious persuasion, wherever "personal efficiency" is a prevailing interest, and in educational circles. The more general the teaching has become, the more difficult is the effort to define it.

Yet, for those of us who have followed its development from within, the New Thought stands for certain typical ideas and methods that may be estimated apart from the admixtures that come and go. The New Thought would have made more permanent headway had its leaders undertaken to estimate it, instead of confining their attention to its direct application, despite all problems and failures. To attempt an estimate is not necessarily to compromise, or to make less use of the affirmative method. One may assess the movement by comparison with other practical and psychological teachings, and thereby find a common ground underlying all points of dispute. What is desirable in the long run is a clear grasp of the principles and methods that bring desired results, whatever the eccentricities of those who have identified the New Thought with favorite side-issues.

Still taking our clue from the history of the movement, let us pass in review certain of the characteristic beliefs and methods. Let us undertake this review with the reminder that any doctrine or method which, like Christian Science, springs by way of radical reaction from former views and methods, must itself undergo restatement before we can make sure that the extreme views have been overcome. In the long run a new movement, such as Protestantism in the days of Martin Luther, may be more notable through what it leads people to think than through the beliefs directly inculcated and widely accepted.

The Silent Method. What are the values of the silent method of treatment and spiritual realization adopted by Mr. Quimby? The adoption of this method has meant for many the discovery of a new line of fruitful investigation leading far beyond the first interests. People who had never thought of looking within themselves to find the causes of their misery, but who had attributed causality to physical agencies, have gained the idea that they are responsible, hence have begun radical reforms. Restoration to health is but one step in this process. The next is to see that the point of view of the inner life involves a psychology of human experience, hence an experiential point of view in contrast with a doctrinal approach to religion. The idea once gained, it is presently applied in all directions, and the doctrine changes from a mere mind-cure to a philosophical interest. Emphasis having once been put upon the higher sources invoked through silence, it becomes a question of silent forces wherever found, hence a matter of the higher resistance (not "non-resistance").

The initial stage in this development has usually involved extreme emphasis on the affirmative power of thought. Thus the influence of heredity, the power of environment, and the potency of all physical forces have been denied. All influences affecting us have for the moment been reduced to those that depend on one's thought concerning them. Thus reasoning, it appears possible to the new enthusiast to do anything they like, eat what they wishes at any hour of the day or night, and in all respects choose their own fortune. Everything is made of the new discoveries concerning the influence of the mind on the body, but nothing is made of the conditioning influences that work the other way. One apparently has no need of eye-glasses or of any other supposed material aid. All aspects of life whatsoever depend absolutely upon the mind's approach to them.

In theory this supremacy of thought is still asserted by many upholders of the New Thought, just as the Christian Scientists stoutly defend the non-reality of any fact lying in their way. But in practice the extreme view has given place to an endeavor to use thought as an agency whenever it can be intelligibly substituted for other powers. Thus the first enthusiasm gives place to a gradual adaptation of life to the new point of view. The effort to purify mental life leads naturally to a desire for purer and simpler food. The moderation of all appetites, the cultivation of a simpler mode of life, naturally follows. Greater interest in outdoor life also comes in some cases. Thus a more rational attitude takes the place of the first assertions of mental independence. Old mental associations are put aside in favor of new hopes and expectations. Habits of life and thought are traced to their causes, and many changes in conduct are made in response to the new ideals. Optimistic anticipations are made to cover the whole of life, that one may look forward to years of increasing usefulness and strength, with waxing instead of waning powers.

Thus independence is fostered in place of the old-time subservience to conventionality. One is encouraged to think for oneself on all matters of moment, and to grant the same privilege to others in open-mindedness, charity, and tolerance. The silent method of seeking help and guidance becomes a clue to any needed knowledge in much the same way that the Quakers seek the "inward light " through silent worship. One is supposed to turn to this resource in full belief that whatever wisdom is needed for the occasion is at hand.

Psychical Experiences. In some cases the practice of silent meditation has opened the door into that strangely fascinating world of psychical experiences in which one is likely to enjoy visions, become acquainted with telepathy, clairvoyance, and clairaudience. A few linger in this region, and identify the New Thought with occultism or spiritism.

Generally speaking, however, the devotees of "the silence" are advised to press on to the stage of communion with God, and to avoid psychical experiences as likely to lead astray.

Mr. Quimby employed the silent method as a means of intuitive diagnosis in connection with spiritual healing, He attributed the insights thus revealed to the divine wisdom. Thus the thought of God was the center, and comparatively little was said about the person save as a medium or instrument. This humility was due to the fact that Quimby was disinclined to take credit to himself. The disadvantage of this attitude is that through constant relationship with the sick, the sensitive, and the nervous, one may become unduly sensitive and self-sacrificing. At this point the New Thought has added a positive contribution to the original teaching.

The Affirmative Method. On the other hand, one may become unduly self-assertive. The tendency of radicalism in the New Thought is to exalt the finite self to the first rank. Thus nearly all the affirmations take their clue from the first personal pronoun, as in the case of the following ideal suggestions from Henry Wood's *New Thought Simplified:* "I am awake to my own divinity," "I have faith," "I affirm my spiritual freedom," "I hear the still small voice," "I have overcome the world, the flesh, and evil. I am pure. I am strong. I am healthy ...I rule bodily conditions." The principle is, to affirm and persistently maintain as *true now* that which you desire, that which is true in ideal only. The advantage is that instead of wavering between what "appears" and what is "real" you positively claim as already true that which is wise and right. That is, what you claim as real is now true of the larger self, the spirit, that part of your total selfhood that is never ill. If necessary, you are warranted in denying whatever apparently stands between you and this ideal. By thus giving the mind unqualifiedly to one idea you exclude every doubt, fear, or negative thought that might arise in protest. Once realize that everything depends upon the ideal put before the mind, and you will not hesitate to claim anything you wish or will to be. The end thus pursued with confidence is the best spur to action. The whole mind tends to give itself to the goal or objective thus resolutely pursued.

This objective corresponds to the reestablished confidence which the wise physician seeks in the re-education of the nervous invalid. The person who can win it for themselves is able to turn the mental tide. Moreover, the affirmative method implies wise use of our subconscious. The appropriate suggestion, impressed on the mind during favorable receptivity, brings after-effects according to the degree of confidence with which the suggestion is instilled. The sick person, or the one who faces failure, is likely to be in a mental state such that it is imperative to outwit the mind by this process -- that is, to depend upon a single positive thought to overcome all negative thoughts. In a more normal state one may not feel the need of outwitting oneself, but may be able calmly to face life's situation, reasoning matters through to the end. It is well to note that, to reason is higher than to affirm, although affirmations may set forces free that are not readily accessible to reason.

The Spiritual Values. In addition to the therapeutic values of the silent method, the habit of meditating on ideals has been for some a means of entrance into real spiritual experience, after they had lost hold of their faith and wandered afield. This is perhaps the most important result of the silent method. People who have sought mental therapists solely to be rid of physical ills, who expressly stated that they did not "wish to hear a word about spiritual thought," have gradually changed; not through the instruction of the healer, but because of the "uplift" experienced during the silent treatment. This experience has convinced them of the existence of higher powers to which the mind is open, they have presently gained some inkling of the mode of receptivity, and have begun to cultivate "the silence" as a means of communion with God. Sometimes the personality of the therapist may have been the decisive factor, and the uplift may have been the influence of an active mind on a receptive one. However this may be, the influence has been attributed to divine sources, and a new interest has been awakened. The resulting beliefs are somewhat as follows:

Each person possesses an inner faculty or God-sense for the immediate reception of divine life. The life thus apprehended is variously made known through intuition, therapeutic power, and other agencies of our spiritual nature, also influencing the mind more directly through the subconscious. The life thus received not only heals but renews, guides, and in every way provides what each person needs. Each of us may be thus renewed and guided; hence each may in a sense become "a law unto themselves." To receive is to be able to give. Accordingly each one may become a healer, may "radiate hope," send out good cheer and love. There are no limits because the resource on which one draws is infinite. The Spirit has created the world. The Spirit through us will create the world anew as we will.

The element of value here is the emphasis put on experience as first in the order of reality, in contrast with the beliefs which have grown out of experience. Each one is counseled to experiment, or live and learn for themselves, each is encouraged to verify spiritual truths in their own person. This brings spiritual realities very near, and makes our spiritual beliefs practical in all phases of life. Again, it means emphasis on inner experience in contrast with the experiences that relate the mind to the outer world. Carried out as a philosophy of religion, this belief in inner experience throws light on the origin of all the great religions, since inner experience is regarded as the same in kind as that enjoyed by the prophets and seers of old.

The Results. What has been the general result of acceptance of this practical optimism? It has been accompanied by a sufficient number of cures and other successes so that it has met with enthusiastic acceptance, and its followers have faithfully lived by it. Gradually they have extended the sphere of their activities to include social reform, and to proclaim the inner method as a universal solvent for all human problems. Some have parted company with the world of fact at this point and have passed over to Christian Science, with its denial that there is any such condition as poverty or evil. Others have modified their views, and admitted the secondary influence of environment. But the majority have held fast to the affirmative method, declaring that "the soul makes circumstance."

One cannot help believing that these disciples of affirmative thought have missed an opportunity at this point. As a class they take little interest in facts, even those that might be said to support their views. No

Estimate

record of cases is kept, no classifications are made. The" Thought" is assumed to be true because it brings results. The percentage of successes is large enough so that failures are neglected. The patient who is restored usually becomes an advocate of the doctrine, and no effort is made to ascertain the precise nature of the trouble in question. The typical devotee turns away from the unpleasant side of life, avoids all sensational and disagreeable news, and endeavors to eliminate all "negative" remarks. What is unfavorable is in general denominated a "shadow," or, as the Christian Scientists would say, "an error of mortal mind." To look back over the road whereon one suffered, in quest of the facts, would be to call up old associations and undesirable mental pictures; hence to be in danger of relapsing into former beliefs. One must not recognize any consideration or influence that might be unfavorable. The central consideration is the cultivation of the good, the realization that we are all perfect children of God. All things, events, experiences, are indeed good when seen in the light of the whole, as spiritual. Hence one should never admit the supposed reality of any fragmentary thing or event.

This affirmative emphasis is due to the fact that the New Thought people are practical workers, untrained in the special sciences, and unaccustomed to accurate observation and inference. It is a new expression of a very ancient principle which underlies our successful undertakings in all fields. When we are determined to succeed we make light of or ignore any possible obstacle. We affirm success, resolutely refusing to admit any such word as failure. Likewise in the human world at large we declare that the right shall prevail, must triumph, despite the apparent injustice of the world. In our individual efforts to conquer undesirable traits, emotions, and other adverse tendencies, we have the best of reasons for identifying the soul with the ideal, affirmatively closing the door whenever the "old Adam" tries to gain the ascendency. The world needs this idealism because there are so many adversities to conquer. We must cultivate it until the last vestiges of Calvinism and other pessimisms have disappeared from the face of the earth.

The Value of Facts. Shall we say, however, that this is the only method that insures success? Note in contrast how deeply our age reveres facts, even the darkest and most disagreeable facts. We believe in penetrating behind the scenes, that we may know precisely how people live. We look for facts and meanings in the events and things themselves. Many a splendid modern reform began when the world for the first time learned the facts about the enslaved, the degraded, and the downtrodden. We have come to believe that the ideal is latent or immanent in the actual and needs to be brought to light. God, we say in modern terms, is "in" the world, re-making it in moral and spiritual fashion. We take little interest in statements that cannot be verified by comparison with facts. What we wish to know is the vital point of the changes even now taking place within and around us. Many would say that natural facts are safer guides than theoretical suggestions substituted for them. Hence they would insist that we return to frank acceptance of life as it appears, with no facts ignored. Our instincts, it would be said, are safer guides than any affirmation; for we might then avoid the illusory beliefs that work mischief with people who undertake to "demonstrate over" nature, on the assumption that there are no powers which the spirit of each person cannot conquer.

However this may be, the New Thought people might have strengthened their position had they carefully collected the facts before and after the cure in great numbers of cases, and classified these according to types. Again, it would have been profitable to make a careful study of failures, inasmuch as a failure is often more instructive than a success. With a sufficient number of cases carefully described, and explained, it might be possible to show what kinds of illnesses and other troubles are most amenable to suggestion. But the difficulty from a New Thought point of view is that no failures should be admitted, lest the therapeutic principle be qualified. The results of a qualified mental therapy are supposedly shown in the case of the Emmanuel Movement, with its dependence on a physician's diagnosis, and its alliance with physiological psychology. From the New Thought point of view, one must believe absolutely in "the supremacy of the Spirit." It is not in any respect a question of fact but solely a matter of principle.

There are undoubtedly respects in which we have permitted the spirit to become subordinate to the body. It may be well to try our wings to see how far we can mount. But the crucial question is: When shall we affirm the human spirit, and when ought we to turn to the divine? When may we safely disregard physical signs and symptoms, and when ought we to adapt ourselves to the order of nature? Apparently, we are conditioned by any number of laws and circumstances not of our own making: Shall we dismiss these as involving no obstacle to human thought? Or shall we regard thought as an agent for wise adaptation to nature's laws and conditions?

The answer is found in the varied experiences of life, according to the temperament of the individual. Some of us are by disposition shy, sensitive, and inclined to overdo in our effort to be truly receptive and humble. For us the lesson of life is learned through wise cultivation of our affirmative mental powers. Others are already so strongly self-assertive that they need to be taught moderation in all their ways. With all of us there are times for waiting, for adjustment, in wise contentment and faith; but also times for surging ahead with confidence. At all times there is reason for believing that we will succeed, and at all times there is reason for adaptation to the conditions and laws whereby success is achieved.

The Value of Suggestion. Suggestion has been defined as "the uncritical acceptance of an idea and its realization in action." It is a hint, intimation, idea, or plan of action insinuated into the mind by a positive impression or indirect association. Its power lies in the fact that it attracts or gathers similar ideas. It is impressed on the mind by means of a mental picture, by repetition, and concentration. In the case of hypnotism it is often enforced by gestures and passes, accompanied by an emphatic declaration. If employed without hypnotism it may be merely verbal, or may be conveyed by thought transference amidst favoring conditions of receptivity on the part of the patient. When employed in self-help it is called auto-suggestion.

The use of suggestion is ordinarily based on the theory that man has two minds, one conscious (objective), the other subconscious (subjective). The conscious mind observes facts and reasons from them to general principles. The subconscious mind does not reason, but receives and registers all impressions and affirmations; it does not forget. The subconscious mind acts directly upon the brain and nervous system, hence directly influences the body; while consciousness possesses no such direct power. By holding an affirmation or suggestion before the mind for a brief period one can so impress the idea upon the subconscious that it will produce after-effects like the suggestion. For it is the function of the subconscious to execute the commands of consciousness. Thus one may command the subconscious mind to awaken the organism at a given hour in the morning. One may in fact issue a command for every possible need. The prime reason is found in the conviction that the subconscious mind is open to an infinite reservoir of life.

The chief difficulty in the use of suggestion lies in the fact that the mind is not always able to give itself to the suggestion. There may be lack of faith or concentration, or a confusion of wants and desires. The method does not appeal to the highly intellectual, but works best among the emotional, sensitive, and credulous. Then, too, counter-suggestions are often operative. A suggestion is effective only in case it is not checked. Our whole habit of life and thought may act as a counter-suggestion. It then becomes necessary to examine one's beliefs and habits in the usual way before the mind is made ready.

It is too much to assume that the subconscious mind has "perfect control of the body." It is well for the highly impressionable that the mind cannot at will produce any sort of change whatsoever through suggestion. A deeper method must be found to reach certain conditions of mind and body not amenable to suggestion.

It is also too much to assume, as Paul Ellsworth does in *The Gist of New Thought*, that the subconscious mind has the power to "take the preponderance of belief, desire, and emotion" and work this mass into the desired bodily expression. For the subconscious mind has no secret or occult power to accomplish what the self is unwilling or unable to do. It is not *bulk* or *mass* that controls us, but character, interest, reason, despite the dead-weight of our unruliness. It is *attention,* not weight, that determines mental after-effects. Consequently, one should depend upon wise selection rather than on hidden assimilation.

It is not then primarily a question of "sinking a requisition into your ·creative center," as if all the possessions you need would come flying to you. To claim that the subconscious mind can "command the infinite spirit" is to forget that this spirit is God, whose wisdom and purposes far surpass our vision. If God has already provided all that we need, we naturally open the mind to receive the gifts that are higher than any of our choosing. On the other hand, our subconscious may well be a willing servant when we have lifted our thought to a high level of desire. The selective process is always conscious. All depends upon what we will to be.

Nor is it desirable to emphasize the contrast between the conscious and the subconscious. We are already *too* widely divided. That is the great human trouble. The ideal is not to continue to outwit ourselves by circuitous insinuation. This is only a device when we are in straits. The method of suggestion does not make for the development of the higher selfhood. If we employ it, let it be for the time until we begin to take a rational view of life. From such a point of view one never likes to enforce an idea that has not fully appealed to one's intelligence. To enter into an idea intelligently is already to accept it, hence it need not be affirmed. The subconscious after-effect will then be the well-known process of assimilation through association.

While, then, it may be necessary or desirable to put the mind into a receptive attitude for the purposes of mental healing, this passivity or amenability to suggestion should not be fostered after the immediate need has passed. One should return as soon as possible into full self-command, alert, thoughtful, even critical. It is no discredit to be unable to receive suggestions. They are most amenable who are credulous, hysterical, sensitive, neurotic, or otherwise abnormal. Thus a high degree of suggestibility opens the door to hypnosis, to mediumship, and undesirable psychical experiences.

This aspect of suggestion has been more clearly brought out by scientific therapists in Europe than by devotees of mental healing at large in the United States. Thus DuBois, for example, in his *Psychic Treatment of Nervous Disorders*, points out the widespread influence of suggestion, and he has made capital use of it in the curing of nervous diseases. The study of psychical phenomena has led him to the promising conclusion that all nervous disorders are curable. Although he is a determinist, and places great emphasis on bodily fatigue and emotional conditions, he finds suggestibility the greatest cause, and not in a way that is creditable to the human self. For it is credulity, anticipated misfortune, mental unsoundness that characterizes nervous people. All nervousness "denotes in the subject who is afflicted with it a mental defect or a characteristic lack of logic." Hence the cure is discoverable, not through the fostering of suggestibility, but the discovery of the mental weakness and its correction through development of the offsetting tendency in the intellectual life.

Thus DuBois concludes that "it is always irrationalism, or the absence of a critical spirit, which encourages us in error. That malicious hobgoblin, auto-suggestion, becomes a part of our life, and works mischief with our days." He quotes Bechterew to the effect that suggestion enters into the understanding by the back stairs, while logical persuasion knocks at the front door. There may indeed be no limit to the power of suggestion. "Human suggestibility ... enters into every act of life, colors all our sensations with the most varied tints, leads our judgment astray, and creates ... continual illusions." Hence the object of true psychological treatment of nervous disorders should be "to make the patient *master of themselves*." The means to this end DuBois finds is the education of the will or reason, the chief characteristic of the will being effort. Therefore to treat nervous disorders one must be a good psychologist and moralist, in order "completely to modify the mentality" of the patient. "The nervous patient is on the road to recovery as soon as they have the conviction that they are going to be cured; they are cured on the day when they believe themselves to be cured." One must therefore know the personality of a patient, the conditions in which they live; and be able gradually to persuade them to adopt a different mode of life. (DuBois pushes far beyond mere suggestion in his later work, *Self-Control and How to Secure It.*)

Estimate

While, then, the term "psychical" means for DuBois the states caused by preceding conditions of mind and brain, with the chief emphasis on the physical organism, his researches look forward to the conclusions we are reaching, namely, that the method of suggestion is of transitory value only. It may be well, in order to break away from bondage to material things, to make all we can of the power of suggestion, trying to raise it to the level of a cosmic energy. But we are likely to be brought to a pause if we think, if we wish to progress.

The tendency of the New Thought, guided by such writers as Thomas Troward and Thomas Jay Hudson, has been to make light of the intellect and of "the objective mind," as if it were undesirable to become intellectual and as if one could have whatever one wishes by "sending out a requisition into the great subconscious." Thus the very power that makes for sanity, that yields knowledge of law and order, is disparaged, and the mind drops back to a lower level. It is time for vigorous reaction in favor of reason and common sense. This is compatible with belief in spiritual intuition and divine guidance. It does not mean the exaltation of the intellect, but its appropriate use as the one power that guards our nature from undue susceptibility.

The corrective of the superficial tendency that has worked its way into the New Thought is discoverable through a return to the method of intuitive analysis employed by Quimby. Mr. Quimby sought through his impressions, supplemented by conversations with the patient, to gain insight into the real inner conditions, the causes of disease and of unhappiness. He did not ignore or gloss over actual conditions. He was not afraid to look at them. Nor did he try to foster suggestibility. His conviction was that "the truth is the cure," that when seen the patient profits by and can be led out of the conditions that caused their misery. The truth to be established in place of the errors was not that of human assertion, not that of finite suggestion; but the divine truth already at hand and implied in the patient's experience, latent in the patient's soul. Hence the efficiency was not human thought, not the "subjective mind," not a mental requisition sent out into the infinite; but the divine power operating through the human self. Hence the patient on their part must *understand* their errors, and endeavor to overcome their credulity by "proving all things, and holding fast that which is good."

Summary. The New Thought has performed a service by steadily calling attention to the powers and influences of thought. Its silent, affirmative method is of great therapeutic and spiritual value. It has called attention to optimism anew and made optimism practical, dynamic. But there has been a tendency to make light of facts, generating theoretical affirmations in their place, and overlooking the lessons to be learned from mistakes and failures. Suggestion is a device by the way, a subterfuge of transitional value. Its use calls attention to the receptive side of our nature, reminds us that we are susceptible, credulous, open to insidious influences. The outcome, however, should not be neglect of the intellect, as if by the law of attraction we could draw whatever we like by commanding "the powers that be" to bring it; not the fostering of the disparity between the subjective and the objective; but the cultivation of illumined reason, the attainment of spiritual understanding. The method of analysis is the corrective of the method of affirmation. We must lay secure foundations to build

Estimate

well. What we need is more knowledge of facts and laws, and more good sense in our thought concerning them.

CHAPTER FIVE

The Mental Theory of Disease

It can hardly be said that even with the experiences of half a century to draw upon the devotees of mental healing have proved that disease is "an error of mind." It has indeed been shown that inner states such as fear, anger, jealousy, worry, excitement, are instrumental in causing disease. The world has assimilated this idea, and the injunction, "Don't worry," has become widely popular. It has also been shown that favorable mental states are of direct assistance in the curing of disease. But it does not follow that the accompanying physical states are merely "shadows." Nor has it been shown that mental treatment is a universal panacea, able to overcome all forms of organic and functional diseases. At best it has been established that suggestion is serviceable in its place, that mental treatment is one more method of healing added to those already possessed, and that spiritual healing can often accomplish results not achieved by merely mental healing. To say this is not to make light of any form of mental healing, but to assign suggestion to its place, study the cases not yet reached, and press on in quest of more wisdom. If suggestion fulfills a function in the allaying of fear and putting the mind into a favorable attitude, it is next a question of the bodily conditions in which changes occur in correspondence with the improved state of mind. For unless physical changes occur also the new state of mind is not far-reaching.

It is clearly impossible to classify all diseases under one head. Some are plainly due to external conditions or accidents, to impurities and otherwise disordered conditions of the body. Others are so largely mental that scarcely any bodily correspondence can be traced. Mental-healing practice shows that in most cases more depends upon the disposition of the individual than on the disease, whether mental or physical in origin. That is, into one's disease there enters one's whole habit of life, its fleshly or spiritual desires, its scattered or controlled forces, its nervousness or its composure. Inasmuch as the whole mode of life is involved in the cause, for example, in the case of nervous prostration, the entire habit of life must be understood and modified to produce a cure. Mental treatment may be instrumental in producing the initial changes, but eventually the process of re-education and adjustment must begin. The therapist can go part way in guiding this process, but the patient must sooner or later take the lead. Thus to take the situation under advisement is to begin a deep study of all the conditions of life. The point attained will depend on the zeal of the lover of health as attainable through wisdom and self-control.

Origin of the Mental Theory. Before we try to supplement the mind-cure, it is well to remember how

The Mental Theory of Disease

the belief arose that all causality is mental. Quimby is responsible for the idea that disease is an "error" or invention. His manuscripts contain many statements that seem to imply that he ignored the bodily conditions of disease and made light of the laws of nature. This is not the case, however. Quimby steadily held to the divine ideal, and insisted that each person had "created their own happiness and misery." What he took exception to was the alleged knowledge of those who judge by appearances, symptoms, and external conditions. This supposed knowledge in the form of opinions, superficial descriptions of disease, and adverse mental pictures acted like "errors" upon the human mind. Thus a sick person is condemned to the servitude of invalidism who might rise into spiritual freedom and health through knowledge of the real self and its powers. ·What is needed is the spiritual or "Christ-science" which gives each person true knowledge of themselves and of their resources. To gain the clue to this knowledge is to be ready to push on into true understanding of life as a whole, to know God as "an ever-present help in time of trouble."

Quimby naturally placed the emphasis on the mental and spiritual factors of life. His view of the world, imperfectly worked out, tended toward a form of idealism. It was doubtless necessary for the mental-healing movement to pass through its period of extreme reaction. But the clue once given, it remains to investigate every possible factor or influence. Thus to assign thought to its proper place would be to make a study of mental life as a whole, in relation to the bodily organism and to the external world. The merely mental theory sprang from "the psychology without a body," above referred to. The resource is to renounce this artificial world of thought in favor of a new study of the mind as investigated by the psychology of the day.

Modern Psychology. Psychology assures us, in the first place, that every mental state has a corresponding condition or event in the brain. This does not necessarily involve a causal connection, as if the change in the brain produced the accompanying mental state, but implies relationship between two series of events, the one psychical, the other cerebral. It is out of the question to describe or to explain the one without the other. One must take into account all the factors of association, instinct, habit, interest, emotion, pleasure and pain, thought, will, in the one case; and the entire nervous and physical systems, on the other. A great deal will depend, to be sure, on the type of modern psychology espoused by way of explanation. This one might proceed in one direction by following Munsterberg, as in his *Psychology, General and Applied*, with his sharp distinction between causal and purposive psychology; and in another direction by following James, with his belief in the interaction of mind and body. But in either case one would find strong insistence on the intimate relationship between mind and brain.

Psychology does not confirm the supposition that thought or the intellectualizing factor of mental life is formative or creative as "the greatest power in the world." Thought appears amidst a variety of processes, and is on the whole less central than will. To understand its function it is necessary to study all our instincts, impulses, and habits; noting the part played by association and memory, the imagination and the emotions. In the end mental life might be seen to be more a matter of the "ruling passion" or "prevailing love" than a question of thought.

A thought or mental picture becomes an actual object of action only in case it be not interfered with by a more influential "ruling passion." No exclusive privilege can be claimed for suggestion. The mere fact that one makes a suggestion, such as "I am healed," however great the emphasis, is no guarantee that it will eventuate in the desired or appropriate physical change. It is followed by the desired result only in case there are other factors at work. The general psycho-physical condition must be taken into account. The individual's habits and modes of reaction also enter in. To ascertain the facts of a mental cure in psychological terms, it would be necessary to know the state of the brain and nervous system, and of the physical organism as a whole, at various junctures. It would then be possible to assign suggestion to its appropriate place.

Psychology finds certain evidences in favor of the existence of the subconscious, but does not support the belief that there is a separate "subconscious mind." It tends rather to coordinate subconscious phenomena with unconscious cerebration, and to explain as many facts as possible in psycho-physical terms. Some of the results achieved under mental-healing practice would appear to be due to the relaxation of nervous and muscular tensions. There is still good reason for cultivating inner quietude, and in every way fostering favorable mental states. But far too much has been assumed with reference to a supposedly wonderful interior mind which will accomplish for us most everything we wish.

It has been uncritically assumed that "the subconscious mind" controls everything in the bodily organism of which we are not directly conscious, hence that by stamping the right suggestion on consciousness any subconscious after-effect that we desire may be secured. This belief implies the further assumption that the subconscious mind touches the body point by point throughout. But this is contrary to fact. Nor can the assumption be made good on the supposition that the brain controls the whole body, and that the subconscious mind controls the brain, hence regulates the entire body. The brain is the only organ directly influenced by the mind, and the brain does not directly control all of the vital functions. For example, the headquarters of the sympathetic nervous system are not in the brain. On the contrary the sympathetic nervous system has been called "nature's great barrier against the whims of the mind ... the physiological safety-break against mental panic in the individual's brain; it is the everlasting safeguard against a demoralized mind." (See Dr. Sadler's *The Physiology of Faith and Fear*) Fortunately for us, therefore, we are unable at will, after a sudden fright, immediately to stop the excited beating of the heart; or at any time to stop breathing by a mental command. Our nervous states interfere to an extent with our breathing and with the beating of the heart, but our excitements are luckily counteracted by the involuntary organism. Before we try Henry Wood's, "I rule the body," we might well ask, therefore, in what respects is it desirable to try to rule the body?

The student of mental healing will miss the inspirational element of the New Thought in a book like Sadler's, but Sadler's more cautious investigations are admirable correctives. For here we have the physiological basis of the influence of the mind on the body, we have due attention given to the emotions in contrast with the usual overemphasis on thought and suggestion. Suggestion is assigned to its place, but the methods of cure turn on understanding and re-education of the will, with a view to self-mastery on the part of the patient.

Habit. A further corrective is found in the stimulating conception of habit now so well known in the terms of William James's famous chapter on the subject in his *Principles of Psychology*. It may be disconcerting to the enthusiast to learn that habit is largely an affair of the brain, hence that many matters can be better explained by reference to unconscious cerebration than by the hypothesis of "the subconscious mind." But it is to the ignoring of this profound fact that many failures are due in the mental-healing world. Many enthusiasts have vainly tried to secure results by suggestion, on the supposition that all habits are mental, when no change could possibly result without knowledge of hidden causes, concealed habits, and a method for eradicating them. A person as "a creature of habit" is an impulsive, emotional, desire-driven animal rather than a reasoning individual. Very few of the conditions against which such a person strives are due to "wrong thoughts." To eliminate the hidden causes of such misery one must know the person as a creature of instincts, passions, sense-feelings, habits; subject to the conflict of desires and emotional or other repressions. To re-educate someone in accordance with ideals of self-mastery, one must show the person how to bring these more hidden activities within the sphere of control; one must teach the person to form new habits to counteract the old. This can best be accomplished through frank admission of the physiology of habit, and wise adaptation to the plasticities and other favorable conditions of the brain.

The fundamental principle of this type of psychology is biological. There is at the basis of the human mind an undifferentiated activity out of which appear in due time the instincts, desires, passions, emotions, and other phases of mental life intimately related to the body. This activity is by nature impulsive, but it tends towards ends, and becomes more and more purposive, as it guards the welfare of the individual. More and more matters are given over to habit as mental life ascends. Mind and body have developed together and are "a mutual fit." It is *will* which after a time becomes the central representative of the original undifferentiated activity. In our efforts at improvement we are, as Dr. J. J. Putnam has forcibly pointed out in his *Human Motives*, far more handicapped by passions, longings, personal cravings for success than we realize. Our promptings when analyzed resolve themselves into two different and apparently antagonistic sets of tendencies, related to our rational aspirations, on the one hand, and to our emotional repressions, on the other. If then we would realize our constructive motives, in contrast to our "motives of adaptation," as Dr. Putnam calls them, we must take into account the fact that we have had a *biological* as well as a *spiritual* history. Egoism, self-love, the "Will to Power" and self-assertion, for example, are stages in our biological history. Will in the sense of conscious attainment is based on reason. Imagination serving the interests of reason is *an attainment.* So is reason in the conscious sense, also disinterested love, which Dr. Putnam puts at the top of his mental scale.

Such a scale gives a mode of classifying "thought" as it at length appears after mental life is well under way. Thought must reckon with the biological history, learn where to strike in. It follows that in studying the influence of the mind on the body we must constantly take the biological history into account if we would rightly place the "spiritual history" with its strivings.

To accept this essentially sound psychology, is to be prepared to modify the mental-healing theory of disease. That is, disease is psycho-physical in origin, and cannot be correctly described or explained in merely mental terms, not even in the case of so-called mental diseases. To understand it we must take the entire structure of habit into account, the mode of life a person has lived, the concealed repressions, the inner conflicts, the history of the sexual instinct. We may pass freely from mind to body, or from body to mind, realizing that the two are inseparable in the life of the disease.

Likewise, the recovery of health is psycho-physical, and is largely due to natural processes, the re-establishment of normal conditions through the operation of the immanent forces of the organism. We note that various co-operative agencies work with nature in the removal of obstructions, and the readjustment of conditions. The removal of nervous tension, for example, is a great help, likewise the overcoming of fear, the allaying of all exciting emotions. More important still is the discovery of the most interior, concealed, or influential cause. But, granted favorable conditions, nature is able to bring about the restorative processes, those that are in any way possible. Even granted that the co-operative agency is the highest angelic source from which a person ever drew power, the therapeutic process must have *a natural basis,* just as all the works of God in the visible world take place in accordance with universal resident forces under precise natural conditions. To say this is not to deprive any therapist of their prerogatives. It is simply to show that whatever the therapist accomplishes is wrought under established conditions.

The Center of Efficiency. Our corrected psychology shows us how and why the will is more directly in line with the immanent activity which sets the healing-process in motion. Thus our attention is turned to a study of the conditions which inhibit and otherwise interfere with the efficient will. Spiritually stated, it is the old-time problem of co-operation between the human will and the divine. Disinterested love, the love of doing good, becomes the prevailing motive, while the mind in general is put in a secondary place. The suggestion or affirmation is secondary. What is called for is not exaltation of the affirmative self but a study of all the factors that impede enlightened reason and the spiritual will. The affirmation or ideal would then be the mental occasion, while the efficiency would rest with the forces wielded. One would avoid side-issues due to ill-founded beliefs in suggestion and the subconscious mind, and endeavor to learn the true nature and place of the human self.

This change of emphasis prepares the way for an explanation of the unusual cures wrought in the pioneer days of the therapeutic movement. It assimilates Quimby's view at its best point, namely, his conviction that the divine wisdom is the real efficiency, and completes the view by indicating a fruitful study into the nature of the divine love. Thus a neglected field once more comes into view, the relationship of the human will and love to the divine will and love. Only by reckoning with the strong self-assertiveness of human nature may we adopt an

The Mental Theory of Disease

attitude leading to the wise use of affirmations, for affirmations take their clues from the more influential prevailing love.

To place emphasis on the combination of thoughts or suggestion, as if a suggestion is necessarily followed by a corresponding process in the functional and organic processes of the body, might be to follow an idea as illusory as that of a young person who, learning something about suggestion, wrote for the "formula for success." The assumption in that case was that by affirmation of a magic combination of words material prosperity would come by a concealed power of attraction, mayhap without work. Now if one be depressed, lacking in confidence, or otherwise disconsolate, a change in thought followed by an improved mental attitude will indeed put a person in a state to work for wealth. The change begins in fact when the possession of wealth becomes the prevailing interest or affection. But the results are favorable only in case the mental change be followed by appropriate efforts and adjustments to the world. The natural conditions, the social and business conditions cannot be ignored. The thought or suggestion is one only of various influential factors. To know what makes thought efficacious one must take the other factors into account.

The same conclusion follows in the case of foods and other substances put into the body. If I hand you a bread-pill, telling you it is an efficient medicine of a well-known type, and if you believe me, you will take it under the supposition that it possesses medicinal properties. On the other hand, if I give you a pill with a powerful drug in it, telling you it is a bread-pill, you will take it with a very different expectation. Now, the results may or may not appear to coincide with the expectation in each case; but if they do, the result does not prove that the sole quality possessed by either pill lay in the thought attached to it. The most that can be proved is that your mental state corresponds with your belief according to your confidence in me. The result produced on your organism by the pill is a matter for physical science to decide. It is absurd to say that foods and drugs are devoid of native qualities. Even if I hypnotize you into the belief that a bread-pill is a drugged pill, so that an effect similar to that which the actual drug would cause is produced, I do not thereby disprove the chemical theory of matter. What I prove is, the power of an affirmation over a mind that accepts it. The mind is indeed a cause in its own realm; but the relation of mental states to physical events cannot be explained on the assumption that thought is the "greatest power in the world."

We have no doubt long stood in need of a practical way to put the mind into the most favorable attitude, so that, in times of illness and sorrow, one shall dwell not on the pain but on the ideals of peace and inner repose which lift the consciousness to a higher level. Granted a mind absorbed in higher things, free from fear and other exciting states, nature can then do the utmost for us. The farther we carry this process, the less need there may be for physical means of aiding nature, the practical outcome being an obedience to nature such as that exemplified by the instinctive life of animals in their complete relaxation when suffering from an injury. But one may adopt this practical method of removing inhibitory states of mind without accepting the mind-cure as a whole. To co-operate with nature is a matter of common sense, and it is well to have the way made plain.

Demonstrations. We have also stood in need of a method by which the spirit may be enabled to triumph over the flesh. No doubt this is what the mental-healing people have sought in their attempts to "demonstrate over" pain and adverse conditions of all sorts. Many have indeed hoped to attain a condition similar to St. Paul's, when he held the viper without harm. But one may well go one mile with them without going twain. There are times when the only sensible course to pursue is to employ physical means; as we do when we have an aching tooth or a broken arm. No one knows just how far the power of the will or spirit may be carried; but most of us would prefer to be conservatively cautious. The supremacy of the Spirit, that is, the "Holy" Spirit, is one thing; while the supremacy of the human spirit or will is another.

Let us say that even in the case of so-called mental diseases such as insanity, the actual disorder is chiefly physical and must be explained in physical terms. For it then becomes a question of removing obstructions and tensions, producing functional and organic changes, when possible; and we know that various methods are effective according to the case. The proper function of thought in the first instance is to discover the root of the trouble, and learn from those who are most competent what should be done. One should be as free to regard the mind as under the influence of the body, as to look for the effects of thought upon the physical organism.

Take the case of fatigue as an illustration of the general principle. As important as it may be to rise above the consciousness of fatigue, giving ourselves whole-heartedly to our work, believing we have power to accomplish what is on hand, it is far more important to know when to make allowances for fatigue, lest one sap life's forces, or permit weariness to color one's mood and affect one's attitude towards the world. For a person might hold their thought aloft in abstract enthusiasm at the expense of their physical welfare, affirming that they are well when they need to know that they are ill. The wise person knows when they have worked long enough, understands that they must rest the organism, and give nature full sway. Accordingly, one adapts one's conduct to the conditions which nature imposes, well knowing that one had not the slightest choice in the arrangement of those conditions. It never occurs to someone to try to "demonstrate over" nature; for we know that to dwell on the mental conditions of life at the expense of the physical, thereby affirming the freedom to work as long as one likes, would be the acme of folly. What one can do with discretion is to work more quietly, without haste, adding to one's efficiency, and making better use of one's energies. But this is a question of the conserving of nervous energy, not of an attitude of mind. One is eager to rid the mind of all illusions, that we may know where we stand, what our actual powers are, and how to use them. So in regard to disease, the wise person would set about to alter the mode or conditions of life which made the disease possible. One's interest is to live rightly, that we may be well. One believes as ardently as the follower of the New Thought, that God meant us to be well; but one declares that the first essential is adaptation to the conditions of normal life.

It is important, then, to guard against a possible misconception. If we adopt the "psychology without a body," ignoring or denying natural conditions, we may create for ourselves an artificial or theoretical world sundered from the real universe. We might then employ merely mental methods, expecting to gain through affirmation what can be won only through physical changes. The danger would be that we might depend on the power of thought when there are serious organic conditions ignored or glossed over. One misconception might indeed follow another.

If, however, we start with the existence of the natural world of law and order, culminating in the human brain as the mind's instrument, we may then study mental life on a scientific basis. The real glory of the human mind would not then be its power to "create" any mental world it likes apart from the world of fact; but that, related to and in a measure conditioned by the brain, the mind may nevertheless triumph over the flesh. There is no difficulty in admitting the powers and functions of the body if we but emphasize the mind's powers under appropriate conditions. We may then freely make use of every such agency as pure food, a favorable environment, plenty of rest, exercise, and sleep; while doing everything in our power to grow in self-knowledge and mental control. The true "demonstration" therefore is not demonstration over nature, but over our own ignorance, our fears, worries, excitements, tensions, constraints, and the rest. When reason begins to reign at the center, the rule of reason can be established all through.

Finite and Infinite. The first misconception of the early enthusiasts was the assumption that thought can accomplish whatever we will, as if it were bodiless. The second point to be guarded against followed from it, namely, that the human individual is the center of attraction. This implies the exaltation of the finite above the infinite, the raising of the human self to the cosmic power. Carried to the extreme, it means putting the finite self above law, nature, and God. Thus one may become affirmative in the extreme, self-satisfied and self-centered. No one is likely to push affirmation to this extreme who takes the matter under serious advisement. But thus to state the case is to realize the need for a right estimate of self-reliance and independence, lest one exceed the bounds of righteousness. One of the best features of the New Thought is its belief in the individual, with one's own higher resources and powers. Its devotees may be pardoned a certain excess if in reacting against the old-time self-effacement they greatly emphasize "the supremacy of the individual," if they react against all bonds and otherwise affirm the self. But in the end there must be readjustment. The ideal is to know oneself as a true child of God, to know humanity from the point of view of the Spirit. In ideal terms we are "members one of another," not isolated units. We are as truly dependent as independent. Our clue is found in the infinite, not the finite. Any exaltation of the individual above the universal must lead to unpleasant reaction.

To declare, then, that "as a person thinketh, so they are," and to take this to mean the thoughts one "holds" or affirms, as if these were more influential than one's prevailing love or will, might be to go off on a tangent for many years. That some have thus taken the principle over-seriously was seen, for example, when members of a New Thought club met to "hold the thought " for the benefit of the sufferers at the time of the San Francisco earthquake. It was also seen when a New Thought leader expressed surprise at the outbreak of the Spanish-American War; for, said he, "I supposed the New Thought had gained a greater hold in this country than that." It is often seen when we find devotees of this teaching steadily "holding the thought" instead of setting to work to educate people in such a way that their affections shall change, and their wills lead to modified conduct.

The tacit assumption underlying this over-emphasis is that thoughts affirmed and sent out will gather their like to such an extent as to be supreme over all other influences. Hence affirmation comes to be the main business of life. If this principle were chief in importance among universal powers, it would then become a question of the societies sending forth the group-affirmations most likely to survive in the struggle for existence. All warfare would eventually become psychological.

It is interesting to find protests against "holding the thought" coming even from New Thought leaders themselves. Mrs. E. Towne in an issue of *Nautilus* answers an inquirer who complains that she has "held the thought for health for several months with very little if any results," by pointing out that this devotee of the mental method has been "holding" the thought instead of allowing it to work. Mrs. Towne shows that the phrase, "holding the thought," is an unfortunate expression since it suggests intense effort and rigidity, preventing realization; and since "holding the thought" is very far from "creating a strong desire" and "tends toward a monotony that kills desire." Then, too, the statement continues, "a great deal that is written about 'holding the thought' gives the impression that action is not necessary; that simply ' holding' a mental image of your desires is all that is needed to bring realization." Instead one should leave the mind "free and responsive to the inflow of creative impulses," one should use set formulas only so long as inspiration comes from them, and should change them frequently.

"When you have clearly formulated your desire, go on about your business and forget all about it for a time. Give the Universal Life a chance to work through you and bring your desires into manifestation."

By pointing out that "holding the thought" is often made an excuse for "real work," and that no one progresses far in using New Thought "unless he is willing to work," this writer touches the root of the difficulty. It is indeed true that "obstacles are not overcome by the use of empty formulas." "The formulas are only an aid to *working out* results along the line of *constructive activity.*" That is, it is the work alone that avails. The formula is merely a plan of action, not a substitute for it. Those who have put the central emphasis on the formula or affirmation have been greatly misled.

Our inquiry has brought us into view of principles which assimilate the truth in affirmationism without assigning thought to the first rank among powers or exalting the finite above the infinite. The emphasis belongs on God and the universe of law and order, and on one's power to know and adjust oneself in attitude and will to the divine purpose. Our clues are found, in the case of each individual, through a study of all the processes that have made us what we are as a mental, moral, and spiritual being. If we have lived a life of excess, no treasury of subconscious ideas affirmed and stored away will buy our release. All depends on the vital center, the heart or will; the actual mode of life or conduct, whatever the protestations. If you shall help someone, everything will depend on your power to lead them into ideal influences and associations, to give them knowledge and aid them so to be quickened that they will wish to conform their conduct to the divine pattern.

The Mental Theory of Disease

The same conclusions follow, if we analyze the method of silent meditation. If the devotee of "the silence" takes their experiences too seriously, they may drop into some of the misconceptions for which mysticism has been notable wherever it has appeared, namely, the exaltation of emotion or feeling as universal at the expense of reason, or the identification of the finite with the infinite.

Religious Emotion. It is well known that no experiences are more deceptive than religious and personal emotions. An emotion flames up for the moment, fills the horizon, and readily runs to excess. It is intimately connected with the impulses, and when one acts from an emotional incentive one is likely to be swept away by the excitement of the moment. An emotion, unless it be the highest love, is seldom a guide in itself, but is of value only when directed towards a worthy object, as in the case of well-moderated loyalty, patriotism, or enthusiasm.

Most of our self-centeredness is emotional, and we are never so personal in the petty sense of the word as when we yield to an emotion, such as jealousy, hatred, or anger. One cannot make much headway in the attainment of inner control without becoming aware of and casting out or transmuting most of the emotions.

Religious emotions are the subtlest of all. The actual feeling, however high its interpretation, may be little more than a sense of general well-being with a vague suffusiveness in which all distinctions are lost. Like all emotions, it has a bodily accompaniment, and in a suffused state the bodily element may readily be mistaken for the spiritual. Hence it is that mysticism, unless touched with unusual purity of heart, so readily lapses into the sensuous and sensual.

Even in the case of the highest religious emotions it is doubtful if the personal feeling, the actual emotion is ever conclusive. Unless skilled in self-analysis, one may easily confuse the feeling with the interpretation read into it. Strictly speaking, the emotional experience is one thing, and the interpretation or theory brought forward in explanation quite another. To say that one "feels" the presence of God, that the soul is "one with God," that one "realizes the Christ within," is in each case to state the result of much thinking, not what one actually feels at the time. Those who differ in interpretation might have substantially the same feelings, psychologically speaking, and yet everything would depend for each upon the theory brought forward. It is the theory that decides, not the experience. The experience is merely raw material for thought. Rightly analyzed it may lead to the conclusion that heavenly powers are immediately related to the soul, powers other than and higher than the fleshly or the mental. It would then be a question of proper discrimination between lower and higher feelings, and of the maintenance of a certain spiritual standard.

Ordinarily the mystical sense of oneness with God which distinguishes "the silence" has led its devotees to a pantheistic idea of God. Hence the affirmation indulged in by some, "I am God." It might be more modest as well as more rational for me to say, "I am deeply absorbed in my own feelings." The resource would be, not to surrender still further to the sense of mystic union, but clear thinking with a view to distinguishing effectively between humanity and God.

There are apparently no values in this new practice of the presence of God that may not be assimilated without lapsing into pantheism. If "the pure in heart" shall see God, if God knows "what things we have need of" even before we ask, we may make our prayers and our worship as concrete and definite as the therapeutic realization of the New Thought and yet give Christianity fresh emphasis. If the world has in a measure lost sight of the therapeutic values of the Christian faith, the resource is to become as filled with the consciousness of the Holy Spirit as were the early Christians upon whom the gifts of healing were bestowed. We may then turn to the New Testament and reread it in the light of this new consciousness, making immediate connection between the realizational silence and Christianity.

Surely, there is no reason to believe that we are separated from heaven and its resources save so far as our own attitude and its attendant conditions are at fault. Seeking the guidance of the Holy Spirit with the firm conviction that it is as intimately present now as at any time in the past, we naturally seek the divine wisdom needed for the specific instance at hand. Thus seeking essentially spiritual help, we lift the self and its processes from the merely mental or personal level to the spiritual. We do not take our own feelings too seriously. We do not try through an effort of the finite will to influence another. We dedicate the finite anew to the purposes of the infinite will. We make no claims concerning our own powers, but seek the Power of powers that we may become ready instruments.

Salvation. The real ills of life are indeed inner, and they call for spiritual healing. It is of the utmost importance to recover the original Christianity in its fullness and place, long usurped because so much emphasis has been put upon sin. But there may still be matters that are sins rather than "wrong thoughts." Moral regeneration of the will may still be a more imperative need than right affirmation. A new expectation, together with the determination to realize one's end and become morally and spiritually free, is essential; and the affirmation of success will carry us part way. But very much will depend on the philosophy of life which affords the affirmation, on our knowledge of what it is that needs to be "saved," and on our idea concerning the Life that saves.

In so far as affirmationism seems to afford a royal road to salvation it must signally fail, as all schemes fail that substitute theory for work. The way of the unquickened is still hard and the steep paths up the mountain of salvation still lie before them. If we have over-emphasized the difficulties, dwelt too much on sin and misery, hell and sorrow, let us with the New Thought give our consciousness to life, that joyous gift which bears us ever forward. If no person "by taking thought" can change the law or conditions of life one iota, everyone by constructively using thought may further the progress of the soul. The ideal is not to ignore the darker issues of life, but to look beyond them to the true light ever ready to guide us into freedom. No genuine Christian would be content to sit in silence in self-complacent optimism, sending out good and pleasant thoughts instead of going forth to learn the real condition of the needy. Where optimistic affirmations begin to reach their limit, the real work of life begins. When encouraged to believe that we should hold our heads erect, that we can change our dispositions, let us seek out the profoundest influences that can uplift the awakening soul.

If over-zealous devotees of the New Thought have made too much of the self, "the old thought" too easily condemned each person as a "miserable sinner."

The Mental Theory of Disease

Through the human personality in any event is mediated everything we feel and know. We cannot escape the human equation, turn where we will. What we need is truer knowledge of just this wonderful being we call the soul: What the mind-curers have done in a faulty way, we can do well by grounding ourselves in knowledge of the hidden processes by which people change from superstition to belief, from fear to doubt, and from doubt to convictions that are worth while. Whatever else is true of us, we have had a mental history; and this must be read by one who would also read the human heart. The best result of the New Thought is that it leads people to investigate, and eventually to press far beyond its initial teachings. Its devotees have pleaded so well for a mental view of life, for affirmation, "the silence, " and the realization of the divine presence, that we are impelled to press forward to a wiser use of these same methods. We need not wrap the mantle of self-assertion about our faces lest pernicious mental atmospheres steal subconsciously upon us. Love is still "the greatest thing in the world," and "perfect love casteth out fear."

CHAPTER SIX

Reconstruction

The greatest merit of the New Thought is that it traces responsibility to the individual, and shows that each of us must begin any desired change or reform by modifying our own attitude and the conduct growing from it. This position has been stated somewhat crudely and superficially by some of its advocates, with undue emphasis on the power of individual thought. It has disclosed side-issues favorable to the development of a new form of self-satisfaction. But we need not dwell on the side-issues. The main point of interest is the new emphasis on the inner life. This gained, we may proceed with our own type of constructive thought, assimilating what appeals to us as sound in fact and principle. In this as in many other new movements there is need of a fresh estimate of the results in the light of problems still unsolved.

The priceless gift of this whole practical movement originating in Quimby's work with the sick is the method of realizing the vital presence of spiritual realities. This method can be assimilated without accepting any of the extravagant claims brought forward by those who permit the cosmos to revolve about the affirmative ego. This is a real contribution to human development. It opens the way for every individual to apply religious and psychological principles to real advantage. It puts the emphasis where every one must place it who learns that inner experience stands first in the order of reality. To test it each has an opportunity to make a distinct advance in the spiritual life -- from believing to doing, from thinking to realizing.

It is very difficult for people who are still devoted to the established usages of organized religion to grasp or employ this method, for the entire system of creeds and authorities stands in the way. Until God ceases to be merely historical, heaven a remote world to be entered only by the duly accredited, and Christianity an authorized system for the benefit of the few, this is likely to remain the case. Meanwhile, for some this direct method of approach to the divine presence is the equivalent of a new revelation of Christianity, this is the great gift of the new dispensation.

Students of the sciences and those who practice psychotherapy usually miss the significance of this method because they penetrate far enough only to seize upon the method of suggestion and the idea of the subconscious mind. Attributing the whole movement to the discovery and use of suggestion, they pass by the religious values of mental healing, and proceed to employ suggestive therapeutics in their own fashion. This is usually done by the aid of "the psychology without a soul," that is, on the basis of determinism, and the entire dependence of the mind on the brain. Thus the average scholar, specialist, or physician who adds mental healing to their list is as far from seeing the spiritual meaning of the movement as those devotees of the New Thought who adopt the "Thought" as a means of making money.

If we turn to recent interpretations of Christianity from a psychological point of view, we find growing recognition given to the inner life, much interest in suggestion and the subconscious mind, but little insight into spiritual healing as an experience. Dr. George Barton Cutten, for example, in *The Psychological Phenomena of Christianity*, interprets the subconscious as equivalent to the old idea of the "heart" as a religious term, and finds that Jesus and the disciples employed suggestive therapeutics. Professor James H. Leuba, in *A Psychological Study of Religion*, is one of the few recent writers on the subject who, instead of discoursing on the errors of Christian Science and missing the values of the New Thought, attributes real significance to the therapeutic movement as a sign of religious growth. Yet Leuba fails to penetrate behind the therapeutic teachings to the practical values for the spiritual life. Dr. W. F. Cobb, in *Spiritual Healing*, has made a contribution to the subject by tracing whatever evidences he can find through the ages that point in the direction of mental healing, and yet his treatise is not one that would lead the reader to explore the subject as of real value to the average individual. Thus a traditionally "religious" person passes by the main interests as readily as the devotee of determinism. The prime difficulty is that the therapeutic movement is judged merely by its teachings, or by Christian Science, and thus the practical method is overlooked.

Various attempts have been made in recent years to write the history of mental healing. All these efforts have sprung out of interest in modern mental healing as practiced since 1850. They have been successful only so far as they have given evidence of mental therapy or something akin to it as a phenomenon likely to occur in any age, not that previous methods and beliefs in any way account for the modern movement. H. Addington Bruce, in *Scientific Mental Healing,* comes nearer the heart of the matter and his statements are correct concerning the American movement. But the author's purpose is to point the way to a study of psychotherapy. His account would be taken as final only in case one were to throw the religious origin of mental healing out of account, finding the New Thought fulfilled in scientific mental healing as practiced in the United States and Europe. No devotee of the New Thought would accept this conclusion. It is a minor matter that interest in mental healing grew out of a study of mesmerism in France. The significant fact is that mental healing arose in the United States in an independent manner, was soon severed from all relationship with mesmerism, and is most directly understood as an expression of the new spiritual age in which we live.

The result has not been essentially different when New Thought writers have sought to explain their doctrine by reference to Unitarianism, Transcendentalism, and liberalism in religion in general. These movements of thought were chiefly intellectual, and were concerned with the transition from an old theology to the views of such leaders of thought as Theodore Parker. These have had a distinctive history up to the present hour, and they have not led in any case to mental healing. Unitarians, for example, have not manifested any more interest in the subject than others. It is experience, not theology or liberalism, which leads to this special interest. Emerson's teachings approach some of the positions maintained by the New Thought, but Emerson did not apply his wisdom to healing, and the practical values in his thought in this direction were not noted until the New Thought came into being. Liberalism in general grew up as independently of mental healing, in the same age, as did spiritualism, sometimes referred to as the movement which alone made mental healing possible.

The Analytic Method. The method of psychoanalysis originated by Dr. Sigmund Freud of Vienna has in many respects led to profounder results than psychotherapy in general. This new method grew out of Freud's investigation of fears, delusions, and fixed ideas, together with the study of dreams. By its application the patient is put through a process of skillful questioning, sometimes aided by the use of significant words, for the purpose of eliciting an account of recent dream-states, hence by inference discovering a clue to the cause of the disease. Patient inquiry eventually brings to light various emotional complexes influential in the production of dreams. These are usually inhibited emotional complexes, those implying ungratified desires and emotions, wishes which have been checked and repressed. Recent occurrences afford subject-matter for the dreams, while the main activity is due to the concealed wish, with its subconscious associations.

Unlike the New Thought healers, Dr. Freud does not find the original cause of a nervous disorder in a hidden "thought," for our hidden thoughts may be superficial in comparison with our unfulfilled wishes. Our conscious thought is in fact so fragmentary and superficial that we may have little realization of the causes of our passing states and long-standing conditions. Our conscious thoughts are mostly determined by our subconscious desires and those activities which make up the life of feeling. We may then be sufferers from a hidden "secret" of which we are totally unaware, because our conventional attitudes lead us to assign intellectual or other causes for our conduct instead of looking deeply into the motor settings of mental life.

Psychoanalysis is employed for the sake of understanding the hidden causes and inhibitions, and bringing them within range of control. That is, it aims at the mastery of the subconscious, although approaching this end with its own special psychology which must of course be understood before one can use Freud's technique. As Dr. C. G. Jung, one of the leaders of the new school, has put it:

> The psychoanalyst's method of working is diametrically opposed to that of the hypnotizer. In direct contrast also to therapeutic suggestion, the psychoanalyst attempts to force nothing on the patient which the latter does not see in themselves, and with their own understanding find reasonable. Faced with the constant desire of the neurotic patient to receive suggestions and advice, the psychoanalyst just as constantly endeavors to lead away from this passive receptive attitude, and to make the patient use their common sense and powers of criticism, that they may with these become fitted to meet the problems of life independently.

Thus the new method is entirely in line with Quimby's conviction that "the explanation is the cure." Quimby discerned the hidden cause by receptively sitting by the patient to gather intuitive impressions through discernment of the patient's "atmosphere." He frequently found the cause in suppressed emotion or unrealized ambition. His studies did not, however, lead him to investigate human emotions and desires at large; hence he failed to develop his discoveries into a method which others could apply who lacked his intuition. Freud's method admirably fulfills Quimby's at the vital point.

In *The Freudian Wish*, a study of Freud's psychology, Professor E. B. Holt points out that the Freudian "wish" is essentially a dynamic concept replacing the idea of "sensation" as the older unit of consciousness, and including all that has previously been classed under the head of concept, impulse, tendency, desire, purpose, attitude, and the like. Thus the motor attitudes of the body, whether they emerge in overt behavior or not, are the will of the individual. The development of character, then, the whole drama of mental life turns on the development of motor setting. Hence the very great ethical importance of the study of wishes in Freud's sense of the term if we would achieve our ends.

What is needed is a profounder study of our biological history, that we may learn at last why we are so backward in our spiritual history. Dr. Ernest Jones thinks that Freud's great work in the field of biological psychology is comparable with Darwin's in his field. Thus psychoanalysis is brought into the field as a study of "the fundamental driving force behind the majority of human activities and interests." This force is in other terms Schopenhauer's *Wille zur Macht*, Bergson's *élan vital* and the "vital impulse" of many other recent writers. The center of interest for all these writers is shifted from the intellectual to the instinctive. For Freud, as described in *Psycho-*

analysis, the center of interest is also shifted from voluntarism to scientific determinism.

Dr. W. F. Cobb, interpreting Freud's results in relation to mental healing in his *Spiritual Healing*, rightly points out that the center of activity is in reality deeper than that of our psychical complexes. A person may, for example, be suffering from the notion that they have committed the unpardonable sin, and may have sufficient reasoning power to see the folly of their fixed idea; and yet they may still be unable to dispossess themselves of their hidden psychical disposition. The important point, in the case of hidden reflexes and concealed psychical dispositions, is the fact that the fundamental Life, which normally would pour its cleansing and invigorating streams through me, finds its road blocked, and can get through only in driblets. From this again result illnesses of many sorts, which form the staple occupation of the medical profession, but are in reality symptoms only of a bad state of the soul. The psychologist, therefore, who, like Dr. Freud, can diagnose from the symptoms of the body their causes in the soul, and can then compel the patient to set to work to counteract their suppressed hallucinations, or dissolve their *idées fixes,* or dismiss their phobia, is in reality applying a spiritual power to disease which, beginning in the patient's spirit, has infected their whole mechanism of living-body. And this is a mode of spiritual healing based on exact and verifiable knowledge of the process by which health degenerates into ill-health.

With profounder insight than Freud's, William James long ago pointed out that the human being is in many respects conventionalized, restrained, inhibited. This is our condition, James showed us, not merely in the case of disease but in general. We are naturally impulsive, freedom-loving individuals, strong in our instincts, given to the life of emotion. By training and through the adoption of creeds we have become over-intellectualized. The result is not only loss of headway in the vital present, but it is seriously a question whether we have energized to the full. The result would be, not mere Freudian analysis to determine the status of our self-restrained organism, but profounder study of psychology of the type set forth by Professor James. This psychology, hard to summarize in a paragraph because of its penetrating insight and scope, is decidedly a psychology of the will in contrast with intellectualism. To study it is to realize afresh the truth in the insistence upon the cerebral conditions of mental life on which the determinists place such emphasis. Yet James is no determinist but a true devotee of freedom. To follow the clues he points out is to be put in possession of the needed facts and principles required to assign human activity to its rightful place. For James has made a masterly study of the phenomena of habit and the laws of attention.

Employing this method of approach we might say that the prime difficulty with us is that old habit-systems survive to contend with the new, so that when we would do good evil is present with us. If, adopting the advice of Professor James, we had kept "the faculty of effort alive by a little gratuitous exercise each day," if we were accustomed to *acting at once* upon an initiative without allowing an exception to occur until we had established a new habit, the state of affairs would be very different. But most of us overlook the fact that there is a receptivity or spontaneity on the psychical side corresponding with the plasticity of the brain through which habits are formed; we forget how our habits were acquired through *paying efficient attention* at the crucial moment, and then launching our activities with vigor. Consequently, we become victims of our own habit-paths, reaping the consequences of early choices. Consequently, Emerson's statement remains true of most of us, namely, that "the step from knowing to doing is rarely taken." With good reason the theologians insist that the problems associated with "sin" are deeper than the problems of disease, for these are connected with our inertias and other habitual resistances, our deep-seated ruling passion. The real question is, How shall one arouse the will so as to touch those deeper elements of our nature which we so readily evade? To accept a teaching which helps us to gloss over the facts and gratify the self by new and subtle devices is still further to postpone the day of reckoning.

The New Thought teachers undoubtedly mean to include the will when they assign so much power to "thought" as the decisive agent. But there is a distinct advantage in differentiating thought from will, and then noting why thought ordinarily makes so little headway. We all know from experience, for example, the difference between merely thinking, imaging, picturing, brooding, contemplating, and actually making an effort sufficient to overcome resistance and establish the desired action. There is also a great difference between putting ideas before the mind of another and actually persuading the other person to "do something about it." It is one thing to allay a person's nervous disorder by suggestion, it is another to induce the patient to change their disposition so that such disorders shall cease. Having traced their irritability and adverse moods to an antagonistic or neurotic disposition, it becomes at last a question of the person's own will. Does the patient care enough about true freedom to undergo the requisite process of interior change? Then let them make that decisive change of heart which quickens love of God and love for others where the love of self ruled before.

We do not evade these deeper issues by changing from a materialistic to a mental view of life, from pessimism to the optimism of affirmations pleasing to the self. We might indeed adopt a new ideal suggestion for each month and by cheerfully holding it before the mind dismiss all disturbing ideas. In the same way we might close our eyes to the darker facts of life, pass by all that is not pleasing in the newspapers, and serenely travel along our chosen highway. But we would simply remain on the same level.

There is, to be sure, no road back to the old self-condemnation, with its emphasis on the weakness of human nature. Nor can we adopt the point of view which so emphasizes the distinctions between the spiritual and the natural, the divine and the human, as to shut ourselves off from divine help. For while we were making sure of all the discrete differences and contrasts, assailing every theory as false which should fail to make our doctrinal distinctions, we would lose headway and become mere doctrinaires. We should then be very near the dangerous position of the exclusive who excludes himself.

Modern thought tends to break down and pass beyond such distinctions. It sees little or no difference between "sacred" and "profane" truth, between revelation and wisdom arrived at through inner experience. It brings God near to humanity, declares that heaven is present now, and sees spirituality emerging from the common life of humanity. Hence the only solution seems to be to keep close to life as directly presented to each one of us, taking our clue from our own deepest strivings. If these strivings afford opportunity for divine help, it is because of God's infinite nearness and the goodness of others. Doctrinal distinctions are of value only in case we use them, without permitting them to use us.

Nor is there any road back to the old form of receptivity. It was once the custom so greatly to emphasize the majesty and power of God, that little was left for the creature save to minimize themselves in the presence of the Creator. The result was an essentially negative attitude, lacking in powers of resistance. In the realm of psychical experiences this negativity meant openness to all sorts of hidden influences and spiritistic forces. In relation to life it meant submissiveness to the divine will, quiescent readiness to take what might come. It implied a weak mode of thought, an inefficient attitude, and a will that struggled to hold itself up to the mark, to the level of unpleasant duty. The New Thought came as the corrective of this abject submissiveness. It substituted self-realization for self-sacrifice, and development for self-effacement. It is nothing if not an affirmative thought, and this positivity has come to stay.

Yet it is impossible to surrender the main point for which the former theology pleaded. However much we make of the finite self we must ever bear in mind that all efficiency is from a single divine source. Neither in spiritual healing nor in the process of regeneration has the human self any independent power. All spiritual life is a sharing of power with its Cause. Our mental processes, realizations, and affirmations are only "occasions" in comparison with true spiritual "causality." The human self is not the decisive agent, the original giver of life, wisdom, and power; it is the instrument to be used, the responsive party. Each must do their part. Each must come to judgment and change their will; but it is "God that giveth the increase."

Is it possible to face two ways at once, so to speak? Can one be strong in one's attitude, affirmative, optimistic, self-reliant, on the alert, efficient, and yet ever bear in mind that receptivity and obedience are essential, that no plan of ours can alter the divine purpose? It would seem so if we believe in the goodness of humanity, anticipate the best, look for success, and in all respects adopt a victorious faith. Each person's part plainly is to act as if from themselves, realizing their individuality, contributing their measure of service to the world, while all the time remembering that they are one among many, that we are "all members one of another" through an Efficiency which realizes heavenly purposes for all.

What is needed, then, in order to avoid the pitfalls into which some have fallen is a more highly developed conception of the self. Instead of starting with thought as the essence of the self, we may well begin with what is sometimes called "the spiritual mind" -- that is, the inmost region which lies open to the inflowing divine life. It is not given us to watch this inflow to determine just where the divine ceases and the human begins. But much depends on our way of thinking about this inmost region and on our thought of the life that comes through it. This is plainly the immediate or intuitive side of our nature in contrast with the intellectualizing function. What we receive intuitively, what we spiritually perceive we later take up into the intellect and the will. That is, life or spiritual experience precedes the idea. The value of ideas is seen in the effort to understand experience. Life or experience also precedes the will. What touches us within is later made manifest through conduct. The highest function of the will is seen in its endeavor to realize in the fullness of conduct that which has touched the soul as heavenly life.

Were we always responsively adjusted to the incoming of the divine life, we would be strong in faith, courageous and affirmative in attitude, at peace with the world, morally sane, physically sound, and abounding in good works for the benefit of others. Our spiritual life is a progress toward this state of adjustment. The tendency of the divine life is steadily to lead us to that goal. Even the tribulations against which we rebel are parts of this movement towards the ideal end. Could we catch the inner vision, we would never rebel, but would accept with contentment whatever the divine tide brings. Our experiences would cease to be hardships to us in so far as we should attain this adjustment.

Thus poised and serene at the center, ready to move forward with the incoming life, we should receive this life as enlightenment in the understanding, and as heavenly affection through the will. The inner life thus illumined, the whole body would be "full of light." To make progress toward this union with heavenly life, what is needed of course is *the idea of it,* together with interior openness or willingness. We may then gradually bring all our thinking and willing into correspondence with it. Without impatience we may follow the course which the divine life takes, instead of insisting upon our own way. To adopt this attitude affirmatively, in the New Thought manner, is to bear in mind that each individual has a right to be, has a work to do. Indeed, the fullest meaning of the divine activity is seen in the fullest and freest development of individuality.

The New Thought and Organized Christianity. Finally, in the process of reconstruction, questions arise concerning the relationship of the New Thought to the organized Christian churches. As already indicated, most of the early devotees reacted against the orthodox churches, and began to establish Sunday meetings of their own. This movement began with the Church of the Divine Unity, in Boston, in 1886, and now includes many societies under different names. Their general character may be gathered from the following statements issued by the National New Thought Center in Washington, for use in Sunday services:

> This organization has for its prime object the teaching of the Christianity of Christ, and not the Christianity of any sect; the doctrine of Jesus of Nazareth, without theological dogma. We believe that Jesus meant just what He said, and that everything that He taught is not only true, but **practical** and **practicable** in daily life. Whenever He is said to have healed, we believe and teach that His cures were effected, not by miracle, or by violation of, or exception to, the laws of his Heavenly Parent, but in compliance with the laws of the Divine. We, therefore, believe and teach that, when the doctrine of Jesus and the Laws of God are studied and followed in daily life, health, happiness, abundance, and healing of the sick "follow them that believe."

STATEMENT OF BEING

There is One Presence, One Intelligence, One Substance, One Life, the Good Omnipotent.

God is the name of the Everywhere Present Principle, in whom I live, move, and have my being.

In all, and through all, and above all, God Almighty.

Thy name is Spirit. I know Thee as the One All-Seeing Mind.

Thou art always with me as indwelling Wisdom and Love.

Thy law is now the Standard of my life, and I am at peace.

I in Thee, and Thou in me.

THE LORD'S PRAYER
(in present tense)

Our God who art in Heaven,
Hallowed is Thy name.
Thy kingdom is come; Thy will is done on earth as it is in Heaven.
Thou givest us each day our daily bread.
Thou forgivest us our debts as we forgive our debtors.
Thou leadest us not into temptation; but dost deliver us from all evil.
For Thine is the kingdom, the power, and the glory, forever and ever.
Amen.

THE NEW DOXOLOGY

Praise God that Good is everywhere;
Praise to the Love we all may share--

The Life that thrills in you and me.
Praise to the Truth that sets us free.
Amen.

The New Church. The Church which might with the strongest reason be claimed as the forerunner of the New Thought is the New Church, for it was Emanuel Swedenborg (1688-1772) as the prophet of the new age who, more than anyone, opened up the whole region of thought since traversed by spiritualists, healers, and psychical researchers. Phineas Quimby had some acquaintance with Swedenborg's views, gained through conversation with a New Churchman in Portland, Maine, and his ideas at certain points are closely in line with Swedenborg's teachings concerning the divine wisdom, the spiritual world, and the life after death. Moreover, Warren Felt Evans, when he visited Quimby as a patient, was a Swedenborgian, and his conversations with Quimby may have made the connections plain. It should be a singularly significant fact to adherents of the New Church that Evans made a radical change from his last Swedenborgian book, *The New Age and Its Messenger* (1864) (published after Evans visited Quimby but evidently written before) to his first mind cure book, *The Mental Cure* (1869), manifesting a great new interest which held him until his death. The former book is a typical exposition of Swedenborg's views; the latter is wholly different in tone. Yet, strangely enough, the devotees of Swedenborg have shown little interest in Evans's career or in mental healing. The reason is undoubtedly found in the fact of doctrinal disagreements. More virtue is found in the acknowledgment of "true doctrines" than in the efforts of the individual to experience the immediate realities of the spiritual world and to live by them. Consequently the therapeutic movement is judged by its "errors and falsities," thus the devotee of Swedenborg misses the value for inner experience of the new practice as we have been studying it in this volume. Granted the errors and delusions, these do not explain the long and persistent life of the new movement. "Pure unmixed error does not live to trouble us long," Professor Joseph LeConte once remarked.

The only way to rid the movement of its crudities is to put aside doctrines altogether for a time, and investigate the therapeutic experience from within, in the light of its spiritual values. William James has taught this lesson with great force in his epoch-making book, *The Varieties of Religious Experience.* From this profound psychological study of religion we learn that there are various relatively independent types of spiritual experience, such as the mystical or the optimistic, each of which may be described by itself. There is no peculiar religious essence, but several springs of religious activity. There is no single religious goal, but a number of spiritual ends. The natural inference is that several systems of interpretation might fit the facts of experience equally well. At any rate, there is no ground for dogmatism. The most promising conclusion is one that leads us to study for ourselves: (1) the various springs of religious experience; (2) the phases of our nature, conscious and subconscious, most active in such experience; (3) the grounds for belief in the near-by presence of the spiritual world; and (4) the practical values of the varieties of religious experience.

In accordance with this scheme, we have been studying the New Thought as one of the varieties. It belongs under the head of what James calls the "Religion of Healthy-mindedness." It has the advantage of being free from belief in miracles and the supernatural, free from religious dogma and authority, and essentially practical in tone. It turns the attention away from human sinfulness, the atonement, and conventional ideas of the future life; and aids people to live the present life well. Thus it may be estimated according to its type, in contrast with other types, as a psychological candidate. It is likely to fall short at points, for all the types are finite. But we cannot estimate it aright unless we learn from within, by the tests of experience, what it constructively stands for.

If we are to look to Swedenborg and his teachings to find a clue to the origin of the therapeutic movement and the reconstruction of the New Thought, it must be sought on an empirical and psychological basis. The singular fact about Swedenborg is not the claim made by his followers that his writings contain a "revelation from heaven," hence that he should be read as a doctrinal authority; but that, led by inner experience, he was lifted into the realities of the spiritual world. He constantly appeals, in his writings, to experience, and teaches that experience of the nearness of the spiritual world is normal. Quite apart, therefore, from his doctrines, one might test this proposition and so trace the relationship between Swedenborg's experience and Quimby's. Given the inner empirical clue, one might then proceed to a comparison of the teachings. The comparison would be singularly fruitful, for Swedenborg's teachings concerning the correspondence between the mind and the body, the spiritual world and the natural, are illuminating, also the accompanying doctrine of "influx" and the explanation of the spiritual causes of disease.

There is a sense, then, in which Quimby and the entire movement of thought which grew out of his teaching may be connected with the "new dispensation" of which Swedenborg was the seer, despite the fact that Quimby does not once quote or refer to Swedenborg in any of his manuscripts, and despite the radical differences of doctrine. If we say that the second coming of the Lord is the disclosure of the inner or spiritual meaning of the Scriptures, we at once find points of impressive resemblance. Quimby did not claim to possess a science of scriptural exegesis, and he was probably wholly ignorant of Swedenborg's *Arcana Coelestia.* But he profoundly believed in the inner meaning of the Bible, and wrote many articles in interpretation of the Gospels, according to his own insights. Like Swedenborg, Quimby thoroughly believed in the immediate guidance of the divine providence, and the efficient nearness of the spiritual world as the source of all our true powers. His practice and his insights led him entirely to discard the former idea of death as a mysterious change in to an unknown world. He said little about spirits, and disavowed connection with spiritism; but he believed in the nearby presence of those who had left this natural plane of existence, and spoke of death as relatively incidental. He taught that each person is a spirit now, not that death will make them so; and he held that there are spiritual "senses" already partly in exercise which each person will fully understand and employ in the future life. These views were the natural implications of Mr. Quimby's intuitive and clairvoyant powers, and the discoveries he made in the inner world of influences to which his insight admitted him. Quimby tended, however, to interpret these influences with reference to each patient's inner world, the "mental atmosphere," and the subconscious mind, which he called "spiritual matter"; and hence he was not inclined to trace such influences to possible groups of good or evil spirits. Out of Quimby's firm conviction of the reality of the spiritual world there grew a strong religious tendency which led to splendid results. Indeed, this may be said to be his greatest gift to his followers. It is possible to trace the growth of his influence without raising the doctrinal questions naturally suggested by the above references to Swedenborg. What is needed, in place of the doctrines, is Quimby's method of realizing the divine presence. If we know that presence as a life, as *dynamic,* we have little need for theology.

Swedenborg lived and wrote in a highly doctrinal age, and he was led to devote much space to the refutation of such doctrines as "salvation by faith," and the theory of the trinity which then prevailed. The New Church was founded in England in 1787 by highly doctrinal people, who emulated Swedenborg as a leader in doctrinal issues. But we live in other times. For us it is inner experience that points the way. With the Society of Friends, we believe in the direct guidance of the inward light. We have learned that spiritual teachings become real and true for us only so far as we empirically and practically verify them. The more directly able we are to turn to the divine guidance and the spiritual world, the less need have we for doctrinal matters. The true Church for us is the invisible, universal Church of the Holy Spirit, of the Living Lord in constant relationship with humanity. For us the great truth of the incarnation is the manifestation of God in humanity. For us the Word of God is both in the inner meaning of the Bible and in "the heart." The light of the new age is everywhere shining, and anyone may be led by its guidance to the spiritual truths of the age. The New Church and the New Thought have both been made possible by the shining of this new light.

CHAPTER SEVEN

Practical Suggestions

Everyone who is trying to live the right life knows that it is one thing to read about a general principle and another to learn how to apply it in daily experience. The world is full of good books, theorists abound without number, but what is needed is the practical incentive which shall send people into the heart of life with new power. The world is also full of people who expect to have every point cleared up intellectually before they begin to live, people who are steadily in search of the book they never will find, namely, one which shall reveal every step of the way so that no thinking will thereafter be required. It is high time to change all this. The change may begin at any time. The way is simple and everyone may follow it. The first step is to turn from theory and from books to life, that thrilling, stirring power that steadily carries us forward.

Let us then keep close to life, and be as little concerned with doctrines as possible, modifying our theory when necessary, if life prove richer than doctrine.

Of course, this statement of the case implies the acceptance of a doctrine as firmly believed in as any other. But what we mean is this, that the true doctrine grows out of life, whereas many put the cart before the horse under the supposition that they can comprehend theories about life before they know life itself.

Summarizing the foregoing chapters, we may state a simple workable philosophy in a few words. There is but one ultimate Power, Life or Being. This whole cosmos, visible and invisible, eternal in the heavens, temporal in space, manifests this one Being whom some call Father, God. Each person has a place and purpose in the cosmos. There is provision not only for each person's life in particular but in relation to all other people. We are members one of another in guidance and in life. To each of us life is made known through desires, strivings, and aspirations. God sends all our experience, not merely the part which we have singled out, through allegiance to some theory, and called "good." It is all good as it comes from God, all meant for our well-being. Our part is to accept it as from the divine wisdom and love.

It does not matter who you are, however serious the problem. Take this principle and apply it. Consider what is going on within you, what is restless, least satisfied, most eager. Do not exclude any part of your life from the divine care, whatever name you may have applied to it in the past, however much you may have condemned yourself. The conflict between the two voices or natures is a part of life, therefore accept it and move forward with it. Give thanks that you are where you are. Let life have you and lead you along. For God is in life, in what you love. You have looked to far for wisdom. You have turned away from the light that was the life of all people.

Taking this principle as your clue, interrogate the heart, considering where you stand and what you need. You can hardly turn thus to life in a reflective manner without learning something of import about yourself. Out of the abundance of the heart you will speak better than you know.

By the heart one means the spirit in each person, the inmost center of life, the center to which we turn in aspiration. Occasionally we are wise enough to turn there first, opening ourselves to see what comes before we ask others. But most of the time we turn to some authority first, or consult tradition.

The Great Question. The question is, Where do you stand today -- physically, intellectually, morally, spiritually -- in your attitude towards the world, in matters of health, in adjustment to members of your family? Can you give answers? Do you know yourself well enough? If not, begin to make this discovery by noting how you live, how you take the little things of life.

In trying to answer, it is a help to consider what your chief desires are, your needs and problems. Ask further, what has brought you to the present point, with just these difficulties and needs. Look back as far as need be (not with regret) to see what you did to bring yourself where you are today. If in conflict, how did it come about? If discouraged, what made you so? If irritated, why? Analyze to determine the more important points. Then as soon as possible begin to concentrate on the ideal. If your own acts brought you where you are, can you not put other activities in motion to bring about the desired results? Think carefully, choose wisely, then cling fast to your ideals when chosen.

The Spirit. Although Spirit (Life) is universal, manifested in all people, meeting the needs of all, each of us must be connected with a special interest in order to realize in full measure the presence of the Spirit, just as one must have a name, an occupation, and much else to enjoy the full benefits of social life. God is manifested to the heart as love, life. Therefore each needs to be expressing love, life, to know God as God is. Each may become aware of the Spirit manifesting its pure essence within their own consciousness.

The Spirit is within every power that touches us, every experience of life. What we need is a way of responding so that we may be led into life. We need to see life as a whole, excluding nothing. It is not necessary to hold affirmatively to one line of thought, as if in fear that an inharmonious thought might disturb the balance. When we look for God in all things, without fear, it will not so much matter what direction we look; for we shall look and live in the Spirit.

The Beginning. The question naturally arises, At what point shall one begin in order to pursue philosophical investigations with direct practical benefit? At the point of greatest need in daily conduct, or the point where the interest is greatest. The point of need is the center of evolution, and to take part in your own evolution in a more wisely conscious way is to discover precisely the practical clues of which you are in search.

For example, you have perhaps dwelt too long in one environment, or lived too long in one household, hence a certain side of your nature has grown at the expense of others. Your problem very likely centers about the understanding and development of due individuality. You may have been subject to a strong personality in the home, hence you have not been self-dependent. Or, again, you have perhaps been far too emotional, subject to the moods and whims of the moment. You have long been a general reader but have read merely what interested you at the time, without systematically assimilating what you read. For all this there is one resource, namely, to begin to understand the play of emotion and the fluctuation of moods by systematic development of the intellectual life.

Temperamental Influences. If there are factors in your life that are mysterious, you will find conditions that are mysterious in the world. If you are one-sidedly developed, your doctrine will be maimed and inadequate. As you are, so is your world. A person may to some extent transcend or make allowances for temperamental and other limitations. But at the outset their vision is colored by these. In the long run their progress must be by means of these conditions, not by avoidance of them. The pessimist must understand or eliminate the sources of pessimism in their life before they can overcome this personal equation in their philosophy of the world; one must understand pain in personal experience before one can see its significance in life as a whole. The pessimist must apply their results individually before they can see their larger social value.

The Need of Self-Knowledge. It matters comparatively little who we are, where we happened to be born, what occupation we pursue, how favorable or unfavorable the environment. For, wherever we begin, the essential is that we awaken to knowledge of the being that we are, and the part we are playing in the world. Whatever we have done, we can now learn its lessons and its laws. Whoever we are, we may become a better self by taking thought for the things of the Spirit. Whatever our occupation, we may make a fine art of it and turn it to philosophic account. It is not primarily a question of physical surroundings, heritage, possessions, vocation, opportunities; but of the philosophic attention we give to what we possess, the value in it for the development of the soul.

Meditation. Under what conditions is silent meditation most profitable? That depends upon the individual and the stage of development. For most of us the best environment is a secluded room, or a quiet place out of doors, in which we may reflect at leisure, during that part of the day when outward circumstances are least intrusive. The early morning hour is preferred by many, while others choose the sunset hour or the late evening. Whatever the time, the first essential is separation from the cares and tribulations of the day. The success of the meditation will largely depend on our powers of concentration -- that is, the ability to throw off care and nervousness, to find the inner center. To meditate in earnestness is to return to yourself, to enter into self-possession and calmness once more. The more marked the self-possession the less difference it makes when we meditate or under what conditions.

Concentration. The best way to acquire concentration is by doing practical or intellectual work with a purpose in view. Someone who endeavors to do their work as well as it can be done learns concentration without thinking of it. To be successful in any undertaking one must analyze -- that is, know details, and combine these into an orderly whole.

Practical Suggestions

Concentration is required to master details; it is seen at its best in organization or unification. Merely to put one's attention on an object or idea and keep it there is to concentrate. A maintained act of will is concentration. Again, to employ the imagination in a constructive or creative manner is to concentrate. To follow a subject logically from premise to conclusion requires close concentration. Concentration, then, is not a power or quality apart from other mental activities, but is a characteristic of orderly or systematic work. The art that conceals art is ordinarily the highest.

Some people try to practice concentration by opening their minds in a vague way, by trying to make the mind a blank. This is the opposite of concentration. True meditation is never a mere relaxation of attention, for this is not progress but reversion. There are times, to be sure, when it is well to browse, to let the attention play about a subject, or for the sake of recovering spontaneity. But it is well to browse while we browse, and when we need to concentrate we should engage in a purposive activity which involves systematic attention.

If you have long indulged in light reading which did not interest you particularly, but merely filled the hour, hence left room for the scattering of attention, forswear all such reading for the time, and devote your best time and thought to that which is genuinely worthwhile. If your attention has wandered, the chances are that what you partly attended to was not worthwhile. Concentrate for a while on that which really interests you and you will not find it difficult to put your mind consecutively on what you are studying. Choose that which interests you most and you will probably find that it will be the most favorable subject for the acquisition of individual power, hence for the deepening of your life's purpose.

Guidance. The question is asked by those who are eager to live by divine guidance, How shall one know the divine leading from the merely human thought? The answer is found in experience. The quality of things divine is empirical and is discovered by trying. Suppose, for example, I wish to make a change in my life and am not sure where and how to begin. If I seek the divine guidance in solitude, it may not come, for oftentimes we know it rather as a check on our actions after we have made a move than as a direct leading. If able to reduce my possible plans to two or three, although still unable to tell which one is right, my best course is to decide on one of these and make a beginning. When in doubt it is not at all undesirable to make all one's preparations to carry out a plan which later is abandoned altogether.

The Leadings Tested. Often times the best reasons we can give for our faith are those that occur to us after an experience has passed, and one would hardly expect to know the reasons in advance. When an entire undertaking has been brought to completion, one can look far back and see any number of reasons for it, and hence obtain light on divine guidance. Many people of faith hold that what we are permitted to do is right, therefore that we can safely infer the divine wisdom from what is done. If allowed to do a thing, I may at least maintain that it was right, since it was necessary that I should bring to the surface whatever factors the deed reveals. These revelations of my inmost self may then show me more clearly how I can follow the divine leadings in the future. If, on the contrary, my action is checked, I shall be able to examine myself to advantage.

Practical Suggestions

The course of action that on the surface plainly appears to have been a mistake may yet have been right in a deeper sense because it was inevitable that one should blunder in order to learn how to succeed. There are mistakes, relatively speaking, and it is well to acknowledge them as such, learning the lessons they teach, admitting one's folly. Yet the mistake that is essential to success is seen in a very different light when one realizes that there were elements in one's nature that had to be expressed before actual headway could be made.

The moral is, set out on some course, do not remain in a condition of uncertainty. Test yourself in the light of the ensuing results. If there are forces within you that must be brought to the surface and exercised first, if there are personal inclinations and temptations, take these as matters of course and reckon with them. For you must know the highway of the spirit, and no one can understand either the direct course or the side issues except through actual experience. No one who deeply longs to be guided will be left without clarifying experiences. The guidance is present even if concealed at the time.

Someone Proposes; God Disposes. I am sitting at my desk writing, with plans for work to cover several weeks. Suddenly, without any warning, I am called away in the midst of a paragraph. Someone has come to ask me to take up the work of another who is critically ill. I see the importance of the opportunity, accept it, and drop my writing for two months. Time shows the wisdom of the sudden change, and I realize afresh the magnitude of the providence of God.

Again, I plan to have a quiet Sunday at home, reading and thinking. The weather grows suddenly colder and I must give attention to the fires and other matters that pertain to household comfort on a winter's morning. I am about to settle down for a quiet hour when someone announces that a little child has wandered from home and is temporarily lost. I go out on a successful quest, and one duty leads to another after my return. Visitors arrive later in the day when at last the hour seems to be favorable. Thus the day passes. But as I look back over the busy hours I realize that a deepened consciousness of oneness with others has come during the day, and the day appears to be richer in result than any I could have planned.

Guidance sometimes comes to us when we consciously seek it, again it intervenes amidst an active day, as if coming out of a clear sky, without any connection with what has gone before. I may not see what is involved in my response, may not see how the experience I now enter into will be completed. What I am led to do may upset many expectations, may run counter to a theory. Nevertheless my part is to respond.

Individuality counts for little save so far as God creates something through it. We are given the power of relative choice, but God is the one efficiency. Personal plans are of little moment unless turned to divine account. It is well to hold all plans in solution, or retain them under the conditions of the railway timetable that is "subject to change without notice."

Poise. Poise is a state of the inner life characterized by faith, peace, restfulness, and accompanied by a balance of forces. It is acquired through the growth of experiences that inspire faith, by mental training, through the realization of ideals, and through habitual spiritual aspiration. It is furthered also through steady endeavor to adjust oneself to the conditions and forces of the cosmos, to adapt the will to the inward promptings that make for growth. Poise can of course be assumed externally for the occasion, and we may gain it in certain respects even while victims of excess in other directions, but what is desirable is repose of character, depth of philosophical conviction, poise as a habit extending throughout the life.

Self-Help. We are able to help ourselves in so far as we have insight into our present condition and see what should be done to remedy it. Of course there are other and temporary means of self-help, but the help that endures is found through self-knowledge, through the wisdom which shows us our real condition and clears away illusions. When we truly understand we need not prop ourselves by employing the devices of denial and affirmation. When we arrive at a goal we need not advertise the fact, but may look about to see what lessons our journey has taught. I really help myself when I take matters home to myself and relate them intelligently to my inmost being. This is true even when the message of helpfulness comes from others, or implies the presence of higher wisdom and love. What I make my own is what remains with me.

Higher and Lower. No fact is more impressive than the contrast between phases of our selfhood which for purposes of convenience may be called lower and higher. The higher stands for ideals, for the attitude of oneness with God. It is "higher" because implying fullness of life, lifting up to unite with love. Yet the term is merely figurative, for one is just as likely to enter into adjustment with the Spirit by settling down in relaxation and receptivity, as by lifting up and out. The lower consists of the old forces whose hold on us has not weakened: habits that enslave, unruly tendencies in our nature, desires that are unappeased, self-will, selfishness.

Experience is in many respects a conflict between these two phases of our nature. There are times when the ideal is uppermost and we are in a triumphant attitude. Times when we move along in a steady way as if there were a balance between the two tendencies. Also times when the lower is reinforced, when all that is unruly is aroused. Now we have a clear sight of the ideal and think that all will be as we wish it, and now we are immersed in the process and all seems dark.

Anxiety. Anxiety usually expresses itself in deeply interior nervous friction which exhausts the energy at a point where it is much needed. The cure for it is found in knowledge of its origin and nature. To be anxious is of course to be inconsistent with professed faith in God. If we believe God is omnipresent, that God cares for all, we must hold that God's providence includes the welfare of the friend or child, for example, about whom we are just now troubled. Anxiety becomes highly emotional, and betrays lack of experience with the world. Children are oftentimes deprived of rightful experiences because of the anxious unwillingness of a parent to have them away from their sight. Thus it implies selfishness and should be distinguished from love. The love which has the good of all at heart is genuinely trustful, and brings peace. Likewise with any undertaking that is worthwhile. One has no time for anxiety who is thoroughly alive to the opportunities which life at its fullness brings.

Life necessarily involves an element of faith or trust. Hence we should be willing to make the venture and forego the worry. We possess power enough to accomplish the tasks at hand. If we fail it will probably be because we have wasted our energies through anxiety. When we are anxious we live in the petty things of life, picking flaws and quibbling. To be trustful is to be open-minded, large-minded, and free.

Sensitiveness. If you are extremely sensitive remember that all powers and conditions may be put to use, and if more responsive than others you should be able to do something which they do not. Moreover, it is well to know that such sensitivity is in part self-centeredness. Therefore if you would be free absorb yourself in service. The extreme subjectivity will disappear when you become filled with what you are doing for others. Finally, remember that this condition is partly due to exaggerated consciousness of sensation. When your health is better you will be less aware of "nerves," hence less subjective, accordingly, much less sensitive.

Readjustment. The painful period which some people pass through the last of September, or in October, after a long vacation in the country, is likely to be merely one of readjustment. This change may express itself in the form of a "cold," as it would ordinarily be called; or in peevishness, a sense of imprisonment, and an interior struggle. Do not mind the nervous and physical conditions, but go about your affairs, take up an interesting form of work and let the readjustment take its course. Other changes of a similar nature occur during the year, for example, when cold weather comes on, or when spring begins. These will have a decreasing effect upon us if we understand them and give ourselves to a higher line of consciousness.

Again, readjustments take place between people, either as a result of drawing closer or because they are pulling apart. If you and your friend are drawing more close in sympathy and affection, take the frictions of adjustment as matters of course, remembering that friendly controversy may bring out important differences of meaning and individuality. If drawing apart you may well consider whether that which has come between is really worth the pain of readjustment. It is inevitable that the interests of those who are making spiritual progress should undergo changes from time to time. The evolutionary process will trouble us very little if we dwell on the goal to be attained.

Temporary Loss of Confidence. The questioner who seeks light on this point would do well to remember that our consciousness is active on various levels and that we sometimes become immersed in mental and physical processes. When I lose confidence, the change is superficial, and I have by no means lost any possession. The depressing circumstance is not myself but is like an enveloping cloud. To judge of my condition aright I must remember what I am at heart, what my blessings are, my purposes in life: I must recall my selfhood at its best estate.

Lost powers are sometimes readily recovered by a fresh start -- that is, by beginning to acquire the habits anew which give expression to these powers. When we recover the initial association we can easily bring the rest to the surface, dispelling the clouds which have obscured our vision for the time being.

Fear. Someone has remarked that "fear is the backbone of disease." This statement is certainly not true of all our maladies, but it may well be pondered with reference to most of them. It suggests that many of our ills are within our control if attacked at the beginning. Worry and anxiety usually spring from

Practical Suggestions

fear, and many of the exciting emotions, such as jealousy, hatred, and anger, are fostered by fear. To destroy our fears is indeed to strike at the backbone of a large number of our disturbing states and bodily conditions. As an emotion, fear is so subtle that it can with difficulty be checked. But fear also possesses an intellectual element and is associated with many of our beliefs, and it may therefore be attacked indirectly. To overcome the idea or object of our fear is to be prepared to conquer the excitement or emotion.

There are, of course, ideas that are worthy of serious consideration, hence it is well to discriminate. Fear was once an instinct of vital necessity in the wilds of nature, where the slightest sound may have been a warning that the individual should be self-protective. But fear has largely outlived its utility in the human world, and in the form of nervous excitement it is ordinarily baseless, a sheer enemy. As an emotion fear grows in the impulsive or excitable person almost as fire burns, consuming the nervous energy with its intensity, ever demanding fresh material. To avoid letting a fear reach this stage, it is necessary to catch it at the very outset. If your fear pertains to your health, remember that the more anxious you become the less likelihood that you will see the wisest course. What is needed is calmness, that you may judge intelligently, and decide what should be done, or command the inner resources which enable you to overcome the trouble in the beginning. Anxiety, gnawing away like a voracious beast, helps to bring about the object of its insatiable desire. On the other hand many fears die away if no attention be paid to them. To share one's fear with a friend may be to drop it immediately, but there are other fears which would have amounted to naught had they never been mentioned. In general, fears take their clue from the general state of the bodily and mental life.

Wisdom Rules It Out. When fear pertains to financial and similar matters, carefully consider the situation before you and decide upon a plan of action, at least a temporary plan which will relieve you of nervous tension. Do not permit yourself to turn the matter over day and night. When you pause to think you soon realize that anxiety carried to bed or borne through the day is exceedingly foolish. It is well, then, to put one's wisdom into practice.

If your anxiety pertains to friends or to members of the family who are nearest and dearest, analyze it to see whether it has the slightest foundation in good sense. Such analysis will enable you to dismiss a part of it as absurd. Then you will probably remind yourself that God still lives, and is as able to protect your friends as yourself. From these reflections you will pass to quiet consideration of the things that need to be done that you may be faithful to your part.

A Practical Philosophy Needed. In each case try to single out the objective of your fear. Then reason it out of being or arrive at a conclusion with regard to it so as to confine it to the intellectual sphere. For fear accomplishes its mischief within us when it gains headway enough to generate excitement or become an anxiety, with all the wear and tear which that word suggests. Fear as a mere idea is amenable to suggestion, maybe banished by thinking, or transmuted so as to be beyond power to work mischief. Hence the advice of the wise who urge us to conquer one fear each day.

Fear of Death Irrational. The fear of death we may as well dismiss absolutely in favor of the new idea of death as a painless transition into a freer state of existence. If we would avoid the fears which in times of great trouble so easily sweep people off their feet, maybe even causing death itself, we may look forward with calm trust to the great transition. It is rather far off any way, for most of us, this transfiguration of the soul; and what we are concerned with when we stop to consider is the productive life of today, with its joys, its blessings, and its privileges. The fear of death is a sort of musty heirloom secreted among possessions which we have never taken out of the attic to dust and ventilate. To expose it to the light of rational day is to see it dissipate.

Inner Friction. If we are rebellious, cantankerous, fretful, anxious, at the center, there will be more or less friction throughout. If nervously intense in our activities at the center, there is likely to be interference with bodily functions all along the line, for instance in the digestive apparatus. On the other hand, if we are at peace within, if contented, trustful, serene, there will be corresponding conditions, especially in the nervous system. To have control and exercise it is to be able to make headway with the adverse conditions and to increase those that are favorable. The life of the organism is always in our favor, for health is natural. The trend of the energy that wells up within us is not merely to preserve us but to enable us to advance.

Inner Freedom. Ideally speaking, a person should be unaware of the functions of their body, unaware that we possess nerves, unconscious of the modes in which the body employs its energies. The best state of health is always a condition of mind and body in which we are absorbed in the end to be attained, thinking not of processes, but of results. That is, health is fullness of life, in the expression of the powers at our command. But health as an attainment is often superior to health as a gift of supposedly favorable heritage. We appreciate what we work for, we truly possess what we are compelled to make our own. It should not then be regarded as a hardship that most of us must give attention to these matters. Willing acceptance of precisely the conditions under which we are placed is no small part of the victory which makes health an attainment.

Incentives. The sufferer from nervousness, ennui, indecision, or restlessness is out of adjustment. If inclined to be self-centered and over-indulgent, if living a luxurious life, with time to waste, and money to gratify every whim, such a sufferer is likely to think that rest is what is required. Once nearly everyone would have said so. Now we know that what is needed is a sufficient outlet for restrained and unused energies, either through work, play, or service. Hence the problem is to find a sufficient incentive, to hit upon some device to compel such a person to be self-helpful. For with the effort made from within, an effort which no one can by any possibility make for another, there follows a round of responses which will lead or prepare the way for freedom if faithfully followed. "Nothing ventured, nothing gained," is a saying with new force in these days.

But the majority are perhaps troubled because of too much work, because of an overmastering sense of fatigue which will not let them think. So they go on from day to day merely doing what must be done, never satisfied, yet always unable to discover precisely why. It is a question of adjustment to the life of the organism. This life is with you whether you spring out of bed with eagerness or force yourself to take up the

Practical Suggestions

duties of the day. You either use it to advantage or disadvantage according to your mood, the incentive that gives you a new start or the slightly adverse condition that takes away your courage. If rebellious, impatient, hounding those who work with or serve you, you will add many superfluous activities to your day, exhausting your energies long before the day is done. But if you begin with thanksgiving in your heart, resolving to be a little more kind, gentle, and loving, you will find that your whole day is different. One day counts for little, to be sure, but it counts. Tomorrow you may add another change to your good resolutions, and the next day find yourself realizing the end you resolved upon the day before. Thus on and on. It is the little changes that avail.

The New Point of View. The great new idea is this: the discovery that all these matters which we once supposed were in the hands of fate, or were merely external conditions, are partly if not largely within our own control; hence that each of us has the power to begin today to be more moderate or more full of life, as the need may be. Health is not only an affair of the whole individual but is in a peculiar degree an individual matter. So far as it lies within our power it is a question of the reactions with which we meet the forces of our environment and the life that wells up or is impeded within us. Our problem is not essentially that of our vocation, of the amount of time at our disposal, or of anything of that sort; but is a question of thought, of the new consciousness which brings the new adjustment. If cantankerous, you are just as good a subject as if you were ever mild and serene. The essential is to put yourself in motion, to let the life that now is possess you more fully. Meet a little more wisely the circumstance which is yours today and you will be one day nearer the freedom for which you long. Evade the issue, and you will postpone the day. Hard seems the law which thus compels us to make effort for ourselves, if we are still looking for salvation from without, or from some miraculous occurrence: beneficent beyond all words does it seem if we realize the mighty opportunities open before us.

Health. Good health is a state of life, and maintains itself through life in an abundantly active, joyous sense of the word -- that is, through changes, new adjustments. Hence to insure it we need to avoid becoming crystallized, rigid, unyielding, mere creatures of habit; since conditions of this sort impede the free play of life. What avails is an attitude of adjustment or obedience to life, whether or not we are at once brought into a state of harmony. For health is a condition of our energies, is a central, fundamental condition; and it may well be that in the effort to attain it in fuller measure we must first encounter impeding habits and other factors that must be brought into line before harmony shall result. In a state of all-round health there is of course peace at the center, hence harmony throughout. But taking ourselves as we are it is well to note that a wiser state of inner adjustment may involve a preliminary reconstruction or regeneration.

There are two points of view from which one's health may be regarded, as a matter which rests with the physician into whose charge one has given it, and as a question that requires individual thought and care. Whatever the external cause of disease, the conditions which forestall or overcome it are within our own power. Our health is also in part dependent on the mode of life we live, the condition of the nervous system as related to our mode of life, and the accompanying frictions, worries, fears, and other emotional excitements. Physicians often advise us in regard to these inner conditions, but it remains for the individual seriously to consider them.

Conditions of Health. It is within our power to go back to the roots of disease, not only in so far as impure and disordered conditions of the body are concerned, but with respect to all the sources that make daily life what it is. If beset by anxiety, high-strung, strenuous, or otherwise immoderate for instance, we may bring about a change by eliminating our fears one by one; by becoming more moderate in all our ways; a little less intense as the weeks pass; more contented with life as it is; and in many other respects free and happy where we were under bondage and miserable. Instead of dwelling on the mental attitudes and states that foster nervousness, we may turn in the direction of better health by endeavoring to be of good cheer, by cultivating equanimity, poise, and inward peace. Thus in place of the rebellious attitude and the pessimism which formerly consumed our substance, we shall as a matter of habit acquire the mental attitudes which are most favorable to the natural conditions of health. Thus a new consciousness in regard to health will be developed, and we shall think of health in mental and moral terms, yet without adopting any of the special beliefs advocated by those who ignore the work of the physician and the care required to maintain the bodily organism.

Health Defined. Looking at the matter in this larger light, let us proceed on the assumption that health is a condition of the entire individual, physical, mental, moral, and spiritual. What interferes with a person's health in any of these respects is likely to interfere with all. What improves one's status in any of these respects is likely to better one's condition as a whole. Someone is in a state of good health who is able (1) to do a fair amount of physical work each day, understanding by the term "work" all forms of physical exercise; (2) to live an efficient life in some direction contributory to human welfare, a really alert, active life, characterized by joy, enthusiasm; and (3) to adapt oneself to one's environment, with its changes in weather, its varying social influences, and the like, in such a way as to maintain an attitude of contentment through daily service by the preservation of spontaneity, sympathy, and love. This statement takes account of the well-recognized fact that idler is happy, that satisfaction in some direction is a necessity, and that altruistic conduct furthers our welfare in a way never equaled by any form of self-centeredness.

Control. To be healthy is to be a law unto yourself as regards the conditions and energies under your control. Control is one of the chief factors of health regarded from within -- that is, control of the brain acquired through systematic training in the field of practical work or of science; and control of the emotions and other mental states which help or hinder the efficient life. Control also involves a degree of freedom, composure, and simplicity such that the energies may be directed to advantage. When someone has control they can check an emotion such as fear, hatred, jealousy; or express one that they will to express because it brings good results, such as love or enthusiasm.

Discard Baseless Fears. There are fears without number that grow out of fatigue and various depleted or high-strung conditions of the organism. These fears will subside with the recovery of normal conditions.

Practical Suggestions

Most of the fears generated under nervous tension and exhaustion are baseless, and it would not be worthwhile to undertake to reason them out of being. Discrimination will in each case enable the sufferer from fear to concentrate on the real causes, leaving all secondary disturbances to run themselves out.

Carry this process of discrimination far enough and it will not be necessary to single out fears as special objects of attack. For with the growth of spiritual understanding one will pursue the mode of life which fosters peace, faith, and efficiency. Once see, for example, that multitudes of fears are inconsistent with your faith and make it a point to live by what you profess and you will no longer find it necessary to give attention to fears of that class. Increase your scientific knowledge of the world, and in the same way you will find your fears dying by whole categories. Transmute your life from anxious affection to positive service and you will realize that most of your anxieties about friends and family were expressions of selfishness, not of self-sacrificing devotion, as you thought. Another category of worries will be blotted out when you begin to take events as they come, rejoicing in all kinds of weather and seeking the good in all things. The growth of philosophical knowledge will also set you free, for it is clearly impossible both to cultivate the essentially philosophical temper and to retain your whims, fancies, and superstitions.

Finally, increase of knowledge in all these directions should bring a directly practical method of self-help, so that when in distress you will know how to proceed. Some have stated the matter in this way: the soul is really never ill, but remains at heart untouched, calm, and free. Fear, together with the excitements and ills that grow out of it, is relatively superficial, and may be regarded as belonging to the nervous system. Therefore to disabuse the mind of its fears one should turn to the idea of the soul as essentially at peace, abounding in trust. To realize that one does not really fear at the center is a great consolation. Sometimes this idea works like magic, and one sees at a flash the utter superficiality of the fear in question. In the same way one can by imagination or by the aid of suggestion separate another person from a fear.

Mastery is the Ideal. It is of little avail to talk about self-knowledge, poise, self-control, the mastery of impulses and emotions, or the art of life in general, unless you yourself have made decided headway in these attainments. If you speak from theory, merely, your lips will belie you. If you have some measure of peace and equanimity, your life shall speak above precept. Therefore when you read about the value of intimate self-knowledge, control of the inner forces and influences, when you are told that the higher power within you can conquer and transmute the lower, there is but one sensible course, namely, direct experiment in your own life. Test the possibilities which are put before you, and you will know from actual experience how far they are genuine.

The question is often asked, Is there a science of the inner life? Assuredly, and each one of us can grasp it and contribute towards its development. How can this be done? By beginning with the facts and experiences at hand, just as we would if concerned with one of the physical sciences. The center of interest for the natural scientist is the laboratory. It is there that the minuter phenomena of nature are studied. The student of the inner life must have their laboratory, also, namely, in their own mind. Instead of recollecting what one has read, or merely depending on tradition, one should proceed to make observations and experiments. To become a philosopher in your own right you must develop the working principles of life from their foundation. You must be even more precise and thorough at certain points, for in the inner world personal predilections are apt to intrude, while the emotions are often sources of illusion.

In performing a chemical experiment, if a foreign substance intrudes, the entire result is vitiated. The chemist must persistently eliminate the sources of error, must take into account all the factors involved, and frequently scrutinize the conclusions to see that no error intervene. Just as the temperature, the conditions of the atmosphere, and the structure of the materials used, must be taken into account by the chemist, so the student of mental life must allow for the factors of heredity, temperament, prejudice, bias, the influences of environment and education, and many other modifying conditions. The venture may not seem worthwhile for the moment. But from first to last one is thereby gaining the most intimate knowledge of human nature. Only by becoming aware of and taking account of all the factors can one hope really to understand.

Our Limitations. It is plain that in our higher science we should not be concerned with the merely "beautiful" side of life. We must know all sides, both excesses and defects, virtues and limitations. If, as Emerson says, "the only sin is limitation," let us acquaint ourselves with our limitations. If our friend be insincere, pray let us know it, and make allowances for it in estimating their doctrine. If, in the absence of facts, our friend has invented them, let us discover precisely how far our friend's theory is genuinely founded on fact. If someone talks foolishly or at tedious length about what they would like to demonstrate, instead of moderately stating what they have demonstrated, let us classify them as a visionary, not as a person of science. Not until we know what a thing is are we likely to see what it ought to be. Better still, knowledge of things as they are is likely to lead to sounder knowledge of that which they may presently become. Error, deceit, insincerity, pessimism, pain, and all forms of evil are interpretable in the light of their evolutionary value. The ideals which are reared on knowledge of facts, in the light of their evolution, are far more likely to be applicable to real life.

The Ideal. What is your total situation? To answer this question adequately is to begin to make fruitful discoveries. To see the purport of these discoveries is to be lifted out of the hampering present into an ideal future. You may wonder if you ever really saw the beauty of the moment until this change of attitude took place. The enjoyment of life has probably increased for you tenfold. With the increase of happiness there has very likely come a greater peace of mind and you are now sufficiently at peace to look about you to see what laws and principles the given conditions teach, when calmly examined.

The totality of the present situation implies far more than this first delightful discovery. It involves the question, What is the character of life in its totality, what is its reality, its purpose? If the self is somehow responsible for these conditions, in part at least, what is the self, what is its essential power, its attitude, its relation to the world of its own consciousness? If one shall accept the present in all seriousness, is it not worthwhile to begin to inquire what is real and what is apparent, that one may adapt one's thought to the true situation? Obviously, it makes a vast difference what theory or system of first principles is accepted. Acceptance of the present implies the endeavor to develop a philosophy of life as a whole.

Character. If we are first to live, then philosophize, we naturally begin with the present regarded as a field for the development of character. Now, character thrives through encountering and conquering obstacles, whereas we were just now trying to run away from our opportunities in search of a world where everything desirable may be had for the asking. Maybe we could not be better placed than we are. What we long for has its price. Here, if anywhere, we may pay the price and receive the reward.

The Wisdom of the Present. For the sake of definiteness, let us lay down the proposition that the present state of the soul, its real situation, is the wisest for the soul. That is to say, there are reasons for dissatisfaction, and yet despite these there is every reason to be grateful for precisely the present conditions, their promise of better conditions soon to be. For if one shall realize the ideals which just now are occasions for dissatisfaction because they are unrealized, the ideal future must grow out of the unsatisfactory present. Taking one's self as one is, the present conditions must be accepted too, for they correspond to the state of development thus far attained. One could hardly expect the conditions to alter until one's attitude shall change, until the present conditions shall have taught their lesson. The respects in which the present situation is most distressing, the circumstances from which one is most eager to be free, may be precisely those which have the greatest blessing in store. Since this is at least a possibility, it is well to overcome all complaint and begin to see the wisdom of the present situation.

This may be a hard saying. But consider the case for a moment. From the point of view of the science of life, what one now is, is the product of what has gone before. Whatever that product is, it is here and must be taken into account. One would rather flee from one's self. One would gladly be what one is not. Yet the future must grow out of the present through gradual modification of it. If to complain, to try to escape from that which causes annoyance is merely to prolong the present, it would appear to be worthwhile to accept the present in its fullness. If one applies this principle where the given situation is most disturbing, the probability is that the entire situation will seem more agreeable.

Have an Ideal. The ideal is to begin each day as if it were literally a fresh creation, going forth to meet a familiar situation with the zest of one who does not know precisely how they shall meet it, or what new interest may intervene. This may sound theoretical in the extreme to those who feel themselves slaves to dull routine, and they may be inclined to be exceedingly scornful. Yet successful workers are not necessarily those who constantly change their outward circumstances or have time to be as leisurely as they like. There is routine in every conceivable work that is worthwhile, and in all work there must be persistent concentration. The successful worker triumphs over circumstance and mere routine by the thought and life which they put into their work. Hence this question we are discussing pertains to the inner world, not to the outer.

Practical Suggestions

I may very well maintain the same associates, attend the same church, and devote my energies to one occupation if indeed I provide for the contrasts, the sidelights, and enlivening incidents which make all this worthwhile, vital. It is not enough to choose one's associates once for all, since they will continue to be genuine friends only in case the relationship is constantly renewed through the experience of doing things together that are worthwhile. If my church be for me a living church, it is because I am contributing something from my own life to it, seeing in it a constant revelation of heaven on earth. My occupation is worthwhile if I make it grow with my growth, or at least learn more from it as the years pass. However many years I may have pursued it, I can make it a new one if each year I endeavor to carry out some aspect of it in a little better way than I did last year.

Fatigue is no doubt a chief cause of monotony and a great many people who believe in variety do not seek it because they are so tired after the day's work is done. But fatigue also grows by what it feeds on, and to change is to rest. If one goes forth to work burdened with the consciousness that the present economic order is wrong, and that one is a victim of the corporations, the weight of the days that have gone will make the present more fatiguing. It is better to do the work of today in and for today, resting at night from the particular day's work. Then when we reflect on the economic order let us make a business of it, and dismiss it after we have thought about it with profit. Then, too, the increase of fatigue depends on the way we work. If we can move about the house, the shop, or office, with a little less tension, a little less nervous haste, we shall not feel so fatigued at the close of the day. If we also take little moments between for thought on ideal things, or for profitable conversation, the day will pass more pleasantly, hence with less fatigue. In every possible situation there is room for thought, hence for variety, therefore for life, and "where there is life there is hope."

Our situation in life need never be one of mere subservience to routine. There is always a way to provide for variety and change if we think far enough back to discover causes. Therefore the opportunity for each is to take the present order of things as we find it, in the first place -- that is, by beginning with ourselves. If you can command times for leisure and recreation, all the better, for you may then plan your life so as to provide for variety in all things. However exacting the situation which you must meet, you will always find a resource by going away from it for a time, then facing it with the new life which change has brought. Likewise with our financial, domestic, intellectual, and religious problems: change, distance, separation, will accomplish what nothing else can. Best of all, the deepest relationships of the heart are strengthened through the occasional days and weeks of separation which unite us to friends as we never can be united if we are always with them.

Monotony and Change. There are multitudes of people in this workaday world who are unaware that the monotony of their daily life is an important factor in their unhappiness. That the routine of work in office or home, factory or mill, is burdensome they may well know and may have learned how to overcome it in a measure. But there is another sort of monotony that weighs upon us even more heavily, the deadening sameness of association with the same people in the same way throughout the months and years. Here is a family, for example, consisting of a father and mother,

Practical Suggestions

a son and daughter who spend nearly all their time at home when not engaged in the daily work outside, and who spend their meal times and evenings in uninspiring conversation on outworn themes. Or, again, it is a business person who lives with their children, none of whom has chosen a purpose in life. At table the affairs of the business world are not discussed because the children are not interested. The latter on their part do not introduce topics from their reading or their social life because the parent would not be interested. In the case of both these families there is a stultifying atmosphere owing to the fact that people who are much alike are too much together. An occasional guest may bring life into such a household, and a summer vacation may make this humdrum existence a bit more tolerable, but for the most part a prosaic monotony steadily prevails.

Sometimes this habitual sameness is due to the fact that a young person of power and promise feels obliged to remain at home with an aged parent when the call of nature or talent would lead such a one into a world of congenial associates. A mistaken sense of duty may keep a person at home evening after evening, and throughout all the holidays or breathing spells, when everyone concerned would be the better cared for if those who are able should take abundant opportunity for change. On principle, the wise young stay-at-home parent goes out of the house every day in the year so that they may be refreshed in mind and body, equipped to do the best for the children. On principle, some families insist that each grown member of the household shall be away from all other members of the family during at least one week each year. Better still, there are households in which sufficient variety is provided for every week throughout the months as they pass, that there may be no accumulation of ennui and fatigue.

It requires but little time and thought to discover an interesting paragraph or page to read at the breakfast table, a bit of information to bring home at noon or night, or an idea of fresh interest that will give zest to the conversation. Life demands sustenance in order to grow and to remain life, life is fostered by change, and if we introduce change into the daily routine the conditions of life are likely to be maintained. The more strong the tendency toward deadening sameness the more effort should be made to break into it with new interests. Something is wrong if there be nothing to say at table, and if no enlivening incidents break into the hours in the library. But to be alive at home means to seek variety outside also, to go to another church occasionally, meet people of various types, attend different sorts of entertainments, or change the form of one's work.

Someone has said that a person should take up a new occupation every seven years. Very few can do this, but the principle is a sound one. In the colleges this principle has long been recognized, and the professor is expected to be absent a year or half year every so often. The person who is alive to the situation may, however, attain the same end by creating their work anew, adopting new methods, or by gaining the inspiration which comes through controversy and contact with people of allied interests.

A Question of Power. Someone asks why, "if God is a God of love and of infinite power," it is not possible for God to "heal all diseases, organic or otherwise? Why limit infinite power?" The answer is that even infinite power works through conditions and according to law. That is, power works through forces and conditions adjacent to, or those that can be brought into relation with, the thing to be affected. In the case of healing, the person must always do their part in some way, through receptivity, through treatment of some sort, or the observance of conditions under which the resident healing power may work. To say this is not in any way to limit "infinite power" but to show how such power expresses itself. On our part the process of obedience and adaptation is a progressive one, according as we understand the conditions which life imposes. Some day we hope so to live that the joints and arteries will not harden. But for many of us this condition is still a remote ideal. Each one can, however, begin to observe better conditions just where they are.

Coordination. If it be not ambition that wears our frames thin, it is likely to be impatience, anger, passion. What if we should seek the creative presence of God within our impulses, considering the way to lift them into productive work for the true, the beautiful, and the good? It may be that amidst these warring elements we possess precisely those needed for creative efficiency, that we are now moving towards their proper coordination. The desire for power or influence, for example, is good. But the prior question arises, what kind of power is worth while in view of the fact that we are children of God? The desires that cause uneasiness are indications that we are active beings and should be about our work. If our restlessness be due to fatigue, if it leads to impatience and anxiety, we would naturally put the organism in prime condition before undertaking to discover desires that are worthy spurs to action. The person who would find peace must make allowances for deflections caused by disturbance of the normal functions, by unusual excitement or fatigue. Really to know one's self is to be able to assign uneasiness and desires to their proper places.

Ambition. It is said to be ambition that kills. Very likely it is, for ambition often implies a nervous, insistent activity which ever drives us to attain what belongs to the distant future, causing misery without limit to its victim. It would be well for the nervously ambitious to consider what is worthwhile, what desires comport with the greatest good to their fellow humans. A mere goading from behind is never a sure guide. The mere expression of desire counts for as little as the inward stress. What is needed is a coordinating system, or scale of values. Enthusiasm is good, but who would be enthusiastic out of order?

Responsibility. It is not necessary to carry the burden of an entire social group or of the whole human race. No person can be productively responsible for more than their own well-played part. The person who has the wisdom to discern their place will be likely to aid others to fulfill their parts instead of goading them. Possibly the powers that are working through us are carrying us towards heaven as fast as we can move. Possibly we are already at heart what we ought to be, but have not yet given the ideal self opportunity to come forth into expression.

The Practice of the Presence of God. If we lift the level of life as a whole we cut ourselves off from adverse influences, and need no longer be concerned with them. The question then is, What enables us to lift the level of life? The practice of the presence of God. Let us start with the idea of the indwelling Spirit as moving in and through all people, making towards the perfection of our natures. The meaning of the contrast and struggle in which we are engaged is the completion of our own spiritual development. The conflict is only necessary until we learn the lesson, make the adjustment. Hence there is no reason to condemn, no reason to wish life were otherwise. We are not tempted above what we are able to endure.

God is with us to enable us to conquer. God is with us as life, within and behind the struggling forces. Let us then practice God's presence by uniting with life wherever we can find it.

The Problem. The problem is to know how to strengthen the ideal phase of our nature so that it shall endure every test, become wholly triumphant, so that there shall no longer seem to be two powers. The end in view is not to suppress or merely hold the lower in check. For the lower is not evil. It is lower in the sense of lesser. The powers that are active within us are good and meant for good. Every desire has its place. What is within and pressing for expression must come out. To suppress is to be under constraint, unnatural, less than our full selves. Freedom comes through fullness of life.

The ideal is to become consistent, unified individuals.

The power that is pent up seeks expression through self-will. But it can be transmuted, used for higher purposes. To undertake to appease a desire on its own level would indeed be to engage in an endless talk. We learn from experience that if the level of life is lifted our desires change and need not be expressed in primitive form. When we change our attitude, for instance, from the desire to get to the desire to give, from the effort to control to the desire to love, then the quality of life is changed.

The resource is to raise the level of our ordinary life. We are well aware that we are reinforced when doubts, fears and impatience come in, and it seems as if evil spirits entered into us, or if someone had influenced us. No doubt we are extremely susceptible. We belong to social groups, and we are influenced by those whose stage of development is like our own. But no influence can take place except through conditions in us which correspond with and invite reinforcing power -- whatever their nature or origin. It is not then necessary to think about supposed evil spirits outside of us. The problem is within.

The Best Attitude. What attitude of thought, will, adjustment, and cooperation best enables us to keep rightly directed? It must be one that embraces the whole of our nature. Note that there must be an attitude of thought, a way of thinking, then an attitude of will by which we enter into active adjustment with the life that is active within us. Then there must be cooperation in our external and social life. First keep the eye centered on the goal, aim very high; for it is our ideal consciousness that lifts us.

www.ingramcontent.com/pod-product-compliance
Lightning Source LLC
Chambersburg PA
CBHW022359040426
42450CB00005B/257